WordPress 2.9 e-Commerce

Build a proficient online store to sell products
and services

Brian Bondari

W9-AWO-306

PUBLISHING

BIRMINGHAM - MUMBAI

WordPress 2.9 e-Commerce

First published: March 2010

Production Reference: 1220210

Published by Packt Publishing Ltd.
32 Lincoln Road Olton
Birmingham, B27 6PA, UK.

ISBN 978-1-847198-50-1

www.packtpub.com

Cover Image by Vinayak Chittar (vinayak.chittar@gmail.com)

Credits

Author

Brian Bondari

Reviewers

Dan Milward

Taeke Reijenga

Acquisition Editor

Usha Iyer

Development Editor

Rakesh Shejwal

Technical Editors

Dayan Hyames

Krithika Sabareeshwar

Hithesh Uchil

Indexer

Monica Ajmera Mehta

Editorial Team Leader

Akshara Aware

Project Team Leader

Lata Basantani

Project Coordinator

Joel Goveya

Proofreader

Joel T. Johnson

Production Coordinator

Shradha Vichare

Cover Work

Shradha Vichare

About the Author

Brian Bondari is a musician, composer, and teacher with equal loves for both music and technology. His hobbies include reading, hiking, composing music, and playing with his pet rabbit. He also spends an exorbitant amount of time lying on the floor grading papers.

Brian earned his doctorate from the University of Kansas in 2009, and is currently an Assistant Professor of Music Theory and Composition at the University of Texas at Tyler. When he is not writing music or grading papers, he serves as Senior Editor for the multi-author technology blog, http://www.TipsFor.us.

You can also visit him at http://www.bondari.com.

There are many people I would like to thank for their help and support while writing this book. First of all, many thanks to Dan Milward and the team at Instinct for their hard work in developing the WordPress e-Commerce plugin, without which this book would not have been possible.

Also, thanks to Usha Iyer, Rakesh Shejwal, Joel Goveya, and other members of Packt Publishing for their help and support during the organization, writing, and editing processes. Additional thanks go to Taeke Reijenga for his work in reviewing the book.

Finally, utmost thanks to my wife Katrina for her unending love, support, and patience.

About the Reviewers

Dan Milward is a 31-year-old self-taught entrepreneur living in Wellington, New Zealand. He enjoys working with WordPress and making games for mobile phones. His earliest "happy" childhood memories are of playing computer games on his Commodore 64/128. If not for the relaxed attitude of his parents around computers and games, then perhaps the WP e-Commerce plugin would never have been made.

Dan and his team have been contributing to the WordPress ecosystem in one way or another for the best part of 6 years, mostly through their work developing WordPress plugins, most notably the world-famous WordPress e-Commerce plugin, which has had over 500,000 downloads.

His company Instinct has an office in Wellington where they focus on making WordPress plugins, and investors in Tokyo where the focus is on user-generated games for mobile phones.

Many people around the world have contributed to the WP e-Commerce plugin but none have contributed as much as Thomas Howard and Jeffry Ghazally. These guys are the real stars behind the WordPress e-Commerce plugin.

I'd like to thank Amber for going easy on me and allowing me to work on this book during "family time". I'd like to thank Jane Wells and Matt Mullenweg from Automattic for all the moral support that they have provided us over the years, and I'd like to thank all the parents out there who allowed their children to play on computers in the 90s. Those children are today's developers and our peers in the WordPress community.

Thank you.

Taeke Reijenga is the co-founder of Level Level, a web design agency from Rotterdam, Netherlands. Level Level focuses on custom WordPress design and development for businesses. Amongst numerous WordPress-based projects are several e-commerce sites build with WP e-Commerce. One of them offers over 100,000 products.

In his spare time, Taeke loves to cook and enjoy a good glass of wine.

You can contact Taeke via `http://level-level.com`

Table of Contents

Preface

So, did you decide to build an e-commerce site using WordPress as the foundation? Wonderful! You've made the choice that more and more people are discovering: that WordPress is capable of far more than just building a great blog. With the extensibility provided by third-party plugins, it can handle almost any task, including powering a growing e-commerce site.

By pairing WordPress with the free WordPress e-Commerce plugin, you can easily create a powerful online store capable of selling a variety of goods, including digital products with automated downloads. It is an ideal combination for hobbyists and small businesses alike. If you have ever dreamed of running your own online shop, or want to add an e-commerce element to an existing physical store, this book is for you.

While installing WordPress and the (WordPress) WP e-Commerce plugin are relatively simple tasks, the work does not stop there. There is still a lot of information that you need to know, and there is plenty to learn about the installation, configuration, payment setup, security, and even design elements. We are going to cover a lot of ground in this book, and by the time we get to the end, you should have a fully functional, powerful, and secure online store at your disposal.

Let's get started, shall we?

What this book covers

Chapter 1, *Getting Started with WordPress and e-Commerce*, provides an introduction to WordPress and the WP e-Commerce plugin, both of which will power our new online store.

Chapter 2, *Getting Ready to Sell*, covers all of the basics of installation and a feature overview. It also covers the essentials of transforming your WordPress installation from a blog into a business-ready platform.

Chapter 3, *Configure Your e-Commerce Settings*, offers a step-by-step walkthrough of all the settings for the WP e-Commerce plugin and lays a solid foundation for creating a catalog of products.

Chapter 4, *Managing Your Product Catalog*, builds upon the preparation done in Chapter 3 and shows you all of the steps necessary to build a product catalog of both physical goods and digital downloads.

Chapter 5, *User Accounts: Customers and Staff*, offers insight into how WordPress handles multiple users and their roles in our upcoming online store, including options related to user registration.

Chapter 6, *Checkout and Payment Setup*, covers the most important element of any online store: getting paid. This chapter provides details on available payment gateways and offers a step-by-step tutorial on setting up both PayPal Standard and Google Checkout.

Chapter 7, *Shipping, Taxes, and Processing Orders*, explores the myriad of options available for getting your product out the door and to the customer.

Chapter 8, *Themes and Design Elements*, provides an overview of customizations with regard to appearance. Topics covered include shortcodes, a CSS overview, and the WP e-Commerce theme engine.

Chapter 9, *Deploy, Secure, and Maintain Your Shop*, shows you how to move from the testing platform to a production server, including watching for any pitfalls that can happen along the way.

Chapter 10, *Alternative e-Commerce Plugins*, explores a range of other plugins that also offer e-Commerce functionality in conjunction with WordPress.

Chapter 11, *Marketing Your Shop*, covers a final, but essential, aspect of running any e-commerce site: ways to make your site known to the world and bring customers through your virtual doors.

Appendix A, *Gold Cart Module Extendibility*, offers a view of available upgrades in the paid modules of the WordPress e-Commerce plugin.

Appendix B, *Setting Up a WAMP Testing Platform*, shows you how to set up a testing ground on your own computer for installing WordPress and all associated plugins.

What you need for this book

For this book, you will need:

- WordPress version 2.9 or above
- WordPress e-Commerce plugin version 3.7.x or above
- FTP software of your choice
- WampServer (optional, but recommended)

Who this book is for

This book is for anyone interested in using WordPress as the basis for a store that can sell physical items, downloads, or services.

It is ideal for a sole proprietor or small business owner with only basic, in-house technical skills. Some prior knowledge of WordPress will help, but is not required. No knowledge of PHP or CSS is expected, but that will also be helpful.

Conventions

In this book, you will find a number of styles of text that distinguish between different kinds of information. Here are some examples of these styles and an explanation of their meaning.

Code words in text are shown as follows: "We can include other contexts through the use of the `include` directive."

A block of code is set as follows:

```
#header {
    background: #73a0c5 url('images/kubrickheader.jpg') no-repeat
bottom center;
    }
```

Any command-line input or output is written as follows:

```
user@yourhost:~$ mysql -h mysql-hostserver -u mysql-username -p
databasename < wp-database.sql
```

New terms and **important words** are shown in bold. Words that you see on the screen, in menus or dialog boxes for example, appear in the text like this: "Once you are finished with the **General Settings**, switch to the **Presentation** tab at the top of the page."

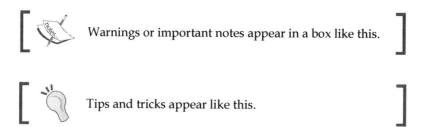

Warnings or important notes appear in a box like this.

Tips and tricks appear like this.

Reader feedback

Feedback from our readers is always welcome. Let us know what you think about this book—what you liked or may have disliked. Reader feedback is important for us to develop titles that you really get the most out of.

To send us general feedback, simply send an e-mail to feedback@packtpub.com, and mention the book title via the subject of your message.

If there is a book that you need and would like to see us publish, please send us a note in the **SUGGEST A TITLE** form on www.packtpub.com or e-mail suggest@packtpub.com.

If there is a topic that you have expertise in and you are interested in either writing or contributing to a book on, see our author guide on www.packtpub.com/authors.

Customer support

Now that you are the proud owner of a Packt book, we have a number of things to help you to get the most from your purchase.

Errata

Although we have taken every care to ensure the accuracy of our content, mistakes do happen. If you find a mistake in one of our books—maybe a mistake in the text or the code—we would be grateful if you would report this to us. By doing so, you can save other readers from frustration and help us improve subsequent versions of this book. If you find any errata, please report them by visiting http://www.packtpub.com/support, selecting your book, clicking on the **let us know** link, and entering the details of your errata. Once your errata are verified, your submission will be accepted and the errata will be uploaded on our website, or added to any list of existing errata, under the Errata section of that title. Any existing errata can be viewed by selecting your title from http://www.packtpub.com/support.

Piracy

Piracy of copyright material on the Internet is an ongoing problem across all media. At Packt, we take the protection of our copyright and licenses very seriously. If you come across any illegal copies of our works, in any form, on the Internet, please provide us with the location address or website name immediately so that we can pursue a remedy.

Please contact us at copyright@packtpub.com with a link to the suspected pirated material.

We appreciate your help in protecting our authors, and our ability to bring you valuable content.

Questions

You can contact us at questions@packtpub.com if you are having a problem with any aspect of the book, and we will do our best to address it.

1
Getting Started with WordPress and e-Commerce

There are lots of great reasons to build an e-commerce website. Perhaps you are a small business owner with goods or services to sell. Maybe you are an author or musician who wants to sell documents, audio files, or other digital downloads. Whether as part of a business, or a hobby, running an e-commerce site can increase your sales, public profile, and your income.

In years past, building an e-commerce site required a vast amount of time, technical knowledge, and money. It meant hand-coding the site from scratch by hiring one or more developers, or purchasing a yearly license for a pre-built e-commerce solution. Surely there must be an easier way. For anyone who starts researching on how to create an online store, the myriad of options seem overwhelming at first. There are literally hundreds of pre-built e-commerce packages available, most of which promise to get the user "running in a matter of minutes". Unfortunately, they also promise to separate the shop owner from hundreds, if not thousands, of dollars. On the other hand, one can also find a few free e-commerce platforms. While most of these are promising, the free cost platform often carries a high price tag in terms of greater complexity or time wasted in learning the ropes of a new platform.

This brings us to WordPress. Not only is it a popular package for building a standard website, but it can also serve as a powerful e-commerce platform with the addition of the WordPress (WP) e-Commerce plugin. Thousands of people have already chosen to use WordPress as the foundation for their online stores, and there are many reasons why you should as well. Yes, WordPress is free, and yes, it's easy to use, but it's also easy to modify and update. Extending the capabilities of WordPress is a breeze, and you certainly do not need a team of developers to get your store up and running.

As we will discover, WordPress is more than capable of handling an e-commerce site. This chapter provides the context for how WordPress fits into the puzzle of e-commerce website construction, what it can do, and why it's so good at what it does.

This chapter covers the following topics:

- Reasons for enabling WordPress for e-commerce
- Some business and website possibilities for the combination of WordPress and the e-Commerce plugin
- What you sign up for when you decide to use WordPress for e-commerce
- A basic overview of the features included in the WP e-Commerce plugin

Why WordPress

Maybe you are attracted to WordPress because it's free, it's easy to use, or perhaps because you have a client who wants to add an e-commerce component to an existing WordPress-based site within the next week. No matter what the case, you need to know a little about what makes it special.

WordPress is free (as in money)

You don't have to pay anyone to use WordPress, whether for personal or commercial usage. Whether you choose to run WordPress on a spare computer in your basement, in a "shared" web hosting environment, or on a cluster of "enterprise-class" servers, there are no licensing fees, support costs, upgrade fees, maintenance fees, or any other kinds of costs.

Most themes and plugins are free as well.

WordPress is free (as in speech)

As an open source project, WordPress makes its code available for anyone to inspect. If it doesn't do what you want, or if you just want to learn more about how certain features work, you are free to poke around the core files and see what makes it tick. You are not only welcome to make any changes or modifications as you see fit, but you are encouraged to do so!

WordPress is widely used

The WordPress project started in 2003. In a few short years, it has grown into the largest self-hosted personal publishing tool in the world. Practically overnight, WordPress has become a household name among the so-called *blogging* software. Contrary to popular belief, it is not just a "blogging" application. While WordPress certainly excels at running personal sites and blogs, it is capable of much more.

WordPress currently powers hundreds of thousands of websites, ranging from personal blogs to Fortune 500 companies, and is seen daily by millions of people. It is likely that you might already be familiar with WordPress.

WordPress is flexible and extensible

One of WordPress' greatest strengths lies in how easy it is to modify and extend. Unhappy with the way your site looks? Try one of the hundreds of user-crafted themes, or have a go at designing your own. The possibilities are limited only by your imagination.

Since WordPress is open source, its functionality is nearly limitless as well. Users have created literally hundreds of plugins to extend its capabilities. If the software does not do what you want *out-of-the-box*, a plugin likely exists to add that functionality. In fact, this book exists because of the extensibility added by the WP e-Commerce plugin.

About the WP e-Commerce plugin

Created by the New Zealand-based *Instinct* Company, WP e-Commerce is an easy and elegant way to integrate e-commerce capabilities into WordPress. The plugin is free (released under the GNU General Public License), though some additional modules are available as part of a paid upgrade.

WP e-Commerce is the product of over four years of development and testing. With over 200,000 downloads to its fame (as of this writing), and featured as one of the most popular plugins for WordPress, WP e-Commerce is the most tried-and-true way to build an online store with WordPress.

It's an ideal solution for selling physical goods, services, and digital products online.

Downloads are available at `http://getshopped.org`.

Site and business possibilities

Just to whet your appetite and get your imagination running, let's take a quick tour to see how people are using WP e-Commerce right now.

Photography shop

If you are an artist or photographer, why not make your product available to the public eye through an online store? WP e-Commerce makes it easy to create listings of your products, complete with sample images. An example of the product listing can be seen in the following screenshot:

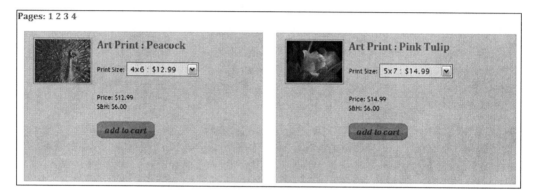

Customers can not only see a preview of your artistic photos, but they can also specify what size print they would like, and the **Price** automatically updates to reflect the differing **Print Size**. The price and size variation option has been used in the intricate art website http://intricateart.com/

Music shop with digital downloads

Perhaps you are a member of a band, a record producer, or a solo classical artist. With WP e-Commerce, it's easy to sell both compact discs and digital downloads of your music. The following screenshot shows the End Up music website:

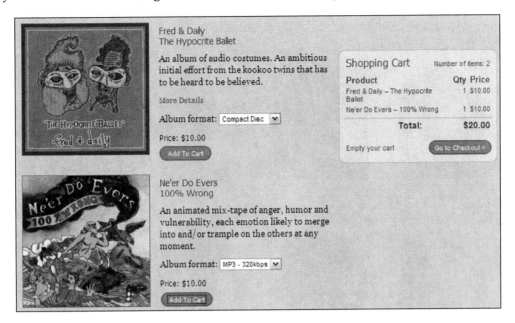

You can provide any sample image for the product that you like, such as album cover art or headshot of the musician. Customers can choose how they want the music delivered, either through a physical disc or by direct digital download. The option of physical disc or digital download has been provided by the End Up music site http://endup.org/.

If customers choose the digital download, WP e-Commerce immediately provides a download link for them. And don't worry, you can restrict the number of downloads allowed by that customer to prevent unauthorized access.

Notice that the **Shopping Cart** in the previous screenshot also provides a running **Total** for this store.

Clothing shop

Maybe you're a small business owner who runs a clothing store, and you want to create an online portal for your store. With WP e-Commerce, it's easy to create a front page that displays a gallery of products (using the optional Grid View module). This can be seen in the following screenshot showing the Seek & Destroy Clothing shop http://www.seekanddestroyclothing.com.

When customers click on a specific product, it takes them to a page with more information. They can also choose a specific shirt size from a drop-down list.

Notice the additional image views that are available, plus the customized **Add 2 Cart** button in the following screenshot:

Accessory shop

Finally, what if you want to sell any other types of goods, such as jewelry or pins? Let us consider the Yay For Pins store `http://www.yayforpins.com`. Here's a unique store. Notice once again that it's easy to create an assortment of products right on the main page of the site, as seen in the following screenshot:

One neat aspect of this store is that it includes the optional DropShop, an AJAX-powered shopping cart that allows customers to drag an item from the page and simply drop it into the cart, which stays fixed and constantly visible in the WordPress footer. This DropShop option is seen in the following screenshot:

In the previous screenshot, notice that there are several products now residing in the cart that is automatically updated to reflect the contents and the total price. Neat, huh?

These are only a few of the possibilities available. No project is too small or large—whether you have one product to sell or 10,000, the combination of WordPress and the e-Commerce plugin can handle it with aplomb. Unless you decide to opt for one of the optional modules, none of the software will cost you a penny.

WP e-Commerce feature overview

Now that we have seen the WP e-Commerce plugin in action, let's take a quick look at some of the overall features.

Organization and layout

WP e-Commerce has a number of features to assist with organizing and displaying of your merchandise. These include:

- Shortcodes
- Tags
- Widgets
- Easy theme integration

Shortcodes, tags, and widgets

Want complete control over the placement of your e-commerce elements? Using tags and shortcodes, you can arrange and display elements in any fashion you desire. For example, adding the [productspage] shortcode to any WordPress post or page will display a list of products from your default product group.

Other tags and shortcodes give you control over the **Shopping Cart, Product Categories**, and **Buy Now** buttons.

Don't feel like digging into the code to arrange elements? No problem. WP e-Commerce also comes with a number of widgets that allow you to graphically arrange the look and feel of your site. For instance, you can set a widget to display **Product Specials**, your **Latest Products**, or simply the location of the shopping cart. The following screenshot shows some of the widgets placed on the sidebar:

Depending on your chosen theme, you can drag and drop those widgets into your theme header, footer, or sidebars.

Easy integration with all WordPress themes

WP e-Commerce does not require any specific WordPress theme. In fact, provided that the theme is designed according to the official WordPress theme guidelines, the plugin should work with all themes.

That said, some themes are more e-commerce friendly than others, and a growing number of themes have been designed specifically with the WP e-Commerce plugin in mind. Naturally, you are welcome to modify or design your own theme.

Some existing WordPress themes deemed to be WP e-Commerce friendly include:

- Copyblogger
- CraftyCart
- Default WordPress theme
- Ferevens
- Fusion
- Gathering
- iTheme
- Light
- Thematic framework
- Textback

Other themes should work as well. If in doubt, just try it.

Products and merchandising

The heart and soul of any e-commerce platform is in how easily and efficiently you can add and manage your inventory. WP e-Commerce gives you full control over your product catalog. You can add a new product directly from the WordPress dashboard, adding any descriptive elements with a rich text editor.

Product groups

Groups are a handy way to help categorize your products. For instance, if you run a clothing store, you can set groups for categories such as t-shirts, pants, jackets, and shoes.

If you sell books, potential groups include fiction, literature, history, romance, and youth.

A photographer might create groups called nature, people, animals, and abstract. You are free to create as many groups as you need. You can even create sub-groups.

Product variations

If you have any attributes that can change for a single product, product variations can come in handy. Variations are options for your products that extend across multiple groups. For instance, a clothing store owner might create one variation for shirt size (small, medium, large, XL, and XXL) and another variation for color (red, green, navy, and black). The product variation for shirt size is seen in the following screenshot:

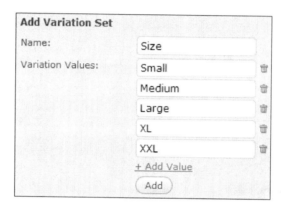

A bookseller might create a variation for the type of cover (hard cover versus soft cover).

A photographer could create a variation for the print size, the finish type, an optional frame, or all of the above. The WP e-Commerce plugin can handle multiple sets of variations for each product, giving customers lots of customization options.

Checkout and payments

What **Shopping Cart** package would be complete without a way to accept orders and payments? In this category, WP e-Commerce certainly doesn't disappoint. The plugin not only keeps track of what items the customer wants to buy, but also calculates additional shipping and handling costs that you specify:

Once the customer is ready to make the purchase, WP e-Commerce collects all of the necessary billing and shipping information on a single page before transferring the order data to the appropriate payment gateway.

Speaking of which, WP e-Commerce allows for seamless integration with a number of payment processors, including:

- Chronopay
- Google Checkout
- PayPal (both traditional and Express Checkout)

Of course, the WP e-Commerce plugin can also handle manual payments, but this opens the door for potential security problems unless you take proper precautions. If you want to manually handle any credit or debit card payments, you will need to have access to the appropriate merchant tools in order to process those payments on your own. In addition, it's strongly recommended that you have an SSL certificate from your web host. If you just want to keep it simple and let one of the aforementioned payment gateways securely handle all transactions, none of those additional tools are required.

Once you start making sales, the plugin maintains a purchase log for you. All transactions are logged on a month-by-month basis. Additionally, you can download a full report as a Comma-Seperated Values (CSV) file for further analysis or financial administration.

Marketing tools

Once your shop is running, WP e-Commerce provides several ways to help promote your products.

Coupons

For starters, you can create coupon codes that apply to either specific items or the entire store. You can also set an expiry time for the coupon, or designate a specific number of usages.

Suggested items

If you enable cross-sales, WP e-Commerce will suggest other items to your customers based on what prior customers bought when they viewed the same product. If you have a large product catalog, this feature is terrific for helping customers find related items.

Integration with external sites

WP e-Commerce generates an RSS feed for your entire product catalog. Provided that you publish the feed on your site, loyal customers can easily subscribe to the feed using any RSS reader. Every time you add a new product to your catalog, subscribers will find out immediately.

On a broader scale, you can also have WP e-Commerce automatically submit your products to Google Base for increased search exposure.

Test platform

Before we begin with the installation and configuration of the WP e-Commerce plugin, let's make one thing clear: I strongly recommend setting up a test platform. You're going to get your hands dirty during this process, and the last thing you want to do is break anything on your production server.

Setting up an e-commerce site is much different from a personal website or blog. Having a testing platform is especially important once we deploy the initial site. Without a testing ground, one little accident or mistake can make your site non-functional, and a broken e-commerce site is of little use to anyone. I implore you not to ignore this warning, and yes, it *can* happen to you, even through no fault of your own. Perhaps a newly installed plugin disagreed explosively with an existing plugin. Perhaps a WordPress update went awry. No matter what the issue, *test all changes and updates before rolling them out to the production server.*

Appendix B covers the setup of a WAMP test server. You can set up WordPress and the e-Commerce plugin on your own computer as a testing ground and try all instructions covered in this book before making a single change to your production server.

Summary

WordPress is a fantastic tool for building a personal website, but it works equally well as the foundation for an online store. Plus, its open nature and extensibility allow for limitless customization and modification.

In this chapter, we covered:

- WordPress' capabilities and familiarities as a tool for both self-publishing and e-commerce
- Some business and website possibilities for the combination of WordPress and the e-Commerce plugin
- What you sign up for when you decide to use WordPress for e-commerce: it's free (in terms of money and speech), extensible, and widely used
- A basic overview of the features included in the WP e-Commerce plugin

The WP e-Commerce plugin harnesses the power and flexibility of WordPress, and seamlessly integrates a **Shopping Cart** into it. Anyone with an existing WordPress installation can quickly add the ability to sell goods and services.

The remaining chapters will walk you through the process of creating and deploying an online store. To demonstrate this process, we will build a sample music store that publishes and sells sheet music in both in physical printed form and electronically via digital downloads.

2
Getting Ready to Sell

Before we can dive into listing and selling our products, we first need to install the WP e-Commerce plugin and then address a few cosmetic and functionality issues. Right out-of-the-box, a default installation of WordPress works great as a typical *blogging* platform, but the needs for an e-commerce site are different. Let's begin work on converting WordPress from a blog-centric platform to a business-focused platform.

This chapter will cover:

- Installing the WP e-Commerce plugin
- Installing third-party themes
- Enabling and disabling comments
- Setting up a static front page
- Using widgets
- Complementary plugins
- Adding a contact form
- Adding a business blog

Installing the WP e-Commerce plugin

At this point, you should already have WordPress installed. If you do not, please visit `http://wordpress.org/download/` to grab the latest version. Some web hosts also offer a one-click install of WordPress via cPanel or another control panel.

Installing the WP e-Commerce plugin is no different than installing other WordPress plugins. There are two ways to do so:

1. Directly from the WordPress Dashboard
2. Manually using your favorite FTP program

Installing from the WordPress Dashboard

This is by far the easiest and most convenient way to install new plugins for WordPress. All you need to do is log in to your Dashboard, expand the **Plugins** menu in the left-hand side column, and click on **Add New,** as shown in the following screenshot:

In the **Search** box that displays on the resulting page, ensure that **Term** is selected as your search option, and perform a search for **e-commerce**. The **WP e-Commerce** plugin should be one of the top results. The following screenshot shows the **Search Plugins** option:

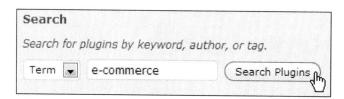

All that's left to do is to click on the **Install** button, and WordPress will handle the rest of the installation for you. The following screenshot shows the search results with the **WP e-Commerce** plugin on top:

Name	Version	Rating	Description	Actions
WP e-Commerce	3.7.5	☆☆☆☆☆	The WP e-Commerce shopping cart plugin for WordPress is an elegant easy to use fully featured shopping cart application suitable for selling your products, services, and or fees online.	Install

Manual installation

If you prefer the tried-and-true method of installing plugins manually, that's also an option. First, download the latest version from:
`http://getshopped.org`

or use the alternate download site:

`http://wordpress.org/extend/plugins/wp-e-commerce/.`

Next, decompress the downloaded ZIP archive with the tool of your choice. We should now have a folder called **wp-e-commerce,** as shown in the following screenshot:

Using your preferred FTP/SFTP program, we need to upload that entire folder to the `wp-content/plugins` directory on your server. See the following screenshot to view the **wp-e-commerce** folder properly uploaded next to a few other plugins:

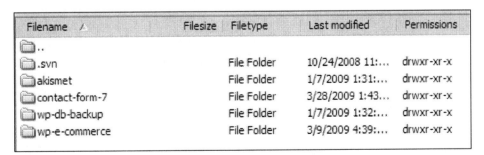

Filename △	Filesize	Filetype	Last modified	Permissions
..				
.svn		File Folder	10/24/2008 11:...	drwxr-xr-x
akismet		File Folder	1/7/2009 1:31:...	drwxr-xr-x
contact-form-7		File Folder	3/28/2009 1:43...	drwxr-xr-x
wp-db-backup		File Folder	1/7/2009 1:32:...	drwxr-xr-x
wp-e-commerce		File Folder	3/9/2009 4:39:...	drwxr-xr-x

The full path to the `wp-e-commerce` directory should be:
`<your WordPress install>/wp-content/plugins/wp-e-commerce/.`

Plugin activation

Now that we have successfully uploaded the plugin, let's activate it. Open your web browser and log in to your WordPress Dashboard. Under the **Plugins** section, you should now see an inactive plugin called **WP Shopping Cart**, as shown in the following screenshot:

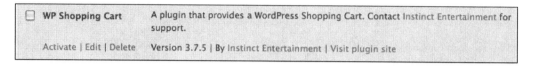

Click on the **Activate** button to enable the plugin. On the left-hand side of the WordPress Dashboard, we now have a new section called **Products**, as shown in the following screenshot:

Congratulations! You have now taken the first crucial step in building an e-commerce site. Let's now continue paving the way for our shop by addressing some functional and cosmetic issues within WordPress.

Installing third-party themes

One of the major strengths of WordPress is how easy it is to customize and alter. This is especially true with regard to themes. If you have the knowledge, experience, and patience to build a theme for your site completely from scratch, you are more than welcome to do so. For the rest of us, it's easy to install and tweak a pre-built third-party theme.

The official site for previewing and downloading WordPress themes is: `http://wordpress.org/extend/themes/`. As of this writing, there are well over 1,000 themes available. Most third-party themes are free, though a number of so-called "premium" themes are also available at varying price levels.

For our upcoming music shop, let's select a free theme. One popular and appropriate option is the **Crafty Cart** theme (`http://bit.ly/crafty-cart`). This theme just happens to be designed with the e-Commerce plugin for WordPress in mind, making it a solid starting point for our shop. Another nice feature is that it's completely free to use for both personal and commercial purposes.

No matter which theme you choose, all third-party themes can be installed in one of the following two ways:

1. Through the WordPress Dashboard
2. Manually via FTP

Installing themes through the WordPress Dashboard

Since the debut of WordPress 2.8, new themes can be downloaded and installed directly through the WordPress Dashboard, just like plugins! The first step is to browse to your Dashboard and expand the **Appearance** menu. Click on the **Add New Themes** link, as shown in the following screenshot:

The resulting **Install Themes** page that loads has a plethora of options for finding and adding new themes. For instance, if you want to view the Crafty Cart theme, just perform a search for **crafty cart,** as shown in the following screenshot:

You can preview and install themes, browse new or featured releases, or filter search results by color, features, or other options. You don't even need to leave your Dashboard if you don't want, which is a welcome improvement over previous versions of WordPress.

Uploading themes via FTP

Of course, the older method of uploading new themes via FTP is still available. To do so, first download the ZIP archive that contains your chosen theme. Go ahead and extract the data within the archive. In our case, the archive for the Crafty Cart theme contains a folder called CrafyCart. If a theme comes with any custom installation instructions, they are usually mentioned in a ReadMe file.

Next, launch the FTP/SFTP program of your choice and log in to your server. Inside your WordPress installation folder, go to the wp-content/themes directory. We now need to upload the extracted folder for our theme to the server. See the following screenshot to view the CraftyCart folder which has been properly uploaded and nested on the server:

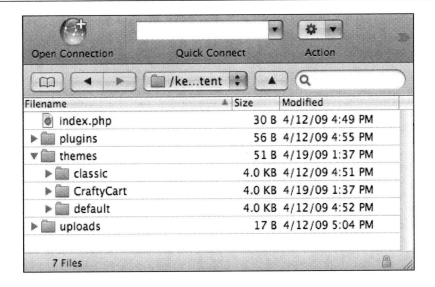

The full path to any third-party themes that you upload should be:
`<your WordPress install>/wp-content/themes/<name of theme>/`.

Activating third-party themes

Once you have added some themes, it's time to activate them. In your Dashboard, scroll down to the **Appearance** section and click on the **Themes** link, as shown in the following screenshot:

You should now see a list of **Available Themes** that you have uploaded, plus your currently active theme. Clicking on an available theme will show a preview of your site using that theme. In our case, we will go ahead and click on the **Crafty Cart** theme. The available themes, including the **Crafty Cart** theme, are shown in the following screenshot:

 Manage Themes

Current Theme

WordPress Default 1.6 by <u>Michael Heilemann</u>

The default WordPress theme based on the famous <u>Kubrick</u>.

All of this theme's files are located in `/themes/default`.

Tags: blue, custom header, fixed width, two columns, widgets

Available Themes

Crafty Cart 1.0.7 by <u>Billion Studio</u>

A Retro Shop Theme designed for the WP e-Commerce Plugin

<u>Activate</u> | <u>Preview</u> | <u>Delete</u>

All of this theme's files are located in `/themes/CraftyCart`.

Tags: two columns, e-commerce, shop, cart, widgets, gravatars

simpleCart(js) 0.6 by <u>Chris Wallace</u>

simpleCart theme.

<u>Activate</u> | <u>Preview</u> | <u>Delete</u>

The template files are located in `/themes/simpleCart`. The stylesheet files are located in `/themes/simpleCart`. **simpleCart(js)** uses templates from **Thematic**. Changes made to the templates will affect both themes.

Clicking on the screenshot of the theme will yield a fully functional preview. When you're ready to commit to a theme, click on the **Activate** button in the top right-hand corner of the preview window. Naturally, some themes are better suited for an e-commerce site than others. Feel free to upload as many different themes as you like, as switching between them literally takes only a few clicks. The following screenshot shows the preview of the theme and the **Activate "Crafty Cart"** option:

Enabling and disabling comments

While the ability to leave comments and interact with readers is integral to the way a standard blog works, it's not nearly as important for an e-commerce site. Unless you have a specific need for comments on your site (such as a business blog), you can disable them entirely. The following instructions will cover how to disable and remove all traces of comments from your site, but you're free to follow only as much as you need, depending on how much customer interaction and feedback you wish to allow. For instance, you may wish to disable comments on WordPress pages, but not on posts, therefore leaving room for comments on a business blog. The choice is up to you.

Disabling comments globally

If you wish to disable comments globally, first enter your WordPress admin panel, scroll down to the **Settings** option within the Dashboard, and click on the **Discussion** link, as shown in the following screenshot:

Once the **Discussion Settings** page loads, look at the top of the page for the **Default article settings**. Deselect all of the checkboxes that allow people to post comments, pingbacks, and trackbacks, and be sure to click on the **Save Changes** button at the bottom of the page. The **Default article settings** options are shown in the following screenshot:

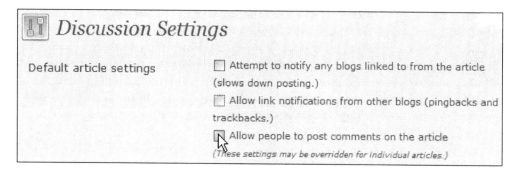

Disabling comments on individual posts and pages

If you decide to leave comments enabled globally, you can still decide to disable them on individual posts and pages. After all, when we create our "Contact" page, how much sense does it make to leave comments enabled on that page? Not much.

To disable comments on individual posts and pages, look for the **Discussion** options when creating the desired post or page. The following screenshot shows the **Discussion** options:

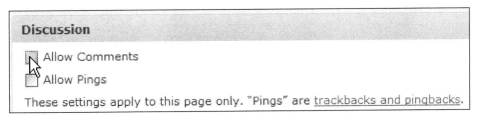

Deselect the checkboxes—**Allow Comments** and **Allow Pings**. Remember that this procedure must be done on a per-post or per-page basis.

Removing comment traces from your theme

Though comments are now disabled, you may notice that your theme still contains references to comments by each post. For instance, our Crafty Cart theme still displays the option to **Write Comment** above each post. The **Hello world!** page is shown in the following screenshot:

You may also see lingering traces such as *No Comments* or *Comments Off*, depending upon your activated theme.

The following steps require the use of a built-in WordPress text editor. You can also connect via FTP and use your favorite full-featured text editor to achieve the same results. Two excellent and free text editors are Notepad++ (Windows) and Smultron (Mac OS X).

No problem. These traces are all easy to remove, though the instructions may differ slightly depending on your theme. First, navigate back to **Appearance** in your WordPress Dashboard and click on the **Editor** link, as shown in the following screenshot:

Next, look on the right-hand side of the Dashboard under **Theme Files** for the files contained within the theme **Templates**. The file that we need to edit is called **Single Post (single.php)**. The following screenshot shows the different **Theme Files** present in WordPress:

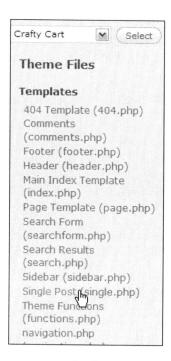

Please make a backup of your theme files before you edit them in case you make a mistake and wish to revert back to the unedited version later.

The first thing we should do is remove the *Write Comment* link from any post using the Crafty Cart theme. Within the **Single Post** file for Crafty Cart, look for this passage of code:

```
<div class="post-footer">
    <h4>
        <span class="post-date"><?php the_time('F jS, Y'); ?></span>
        <span class="post-comments"><a href="<?php comments_link();
          ?>" title="See comments for this post">
        <?php comments_number('Write Comment','1 Comment',
                        '% Comments'); ?></a></span>
        <span class="post-category"><?php the_category(' &middot; ');
          ?></span>
        <?php the_tags('<br/><span class="post-tags">Tags: ', ', ',
          '</span>'); ?>
    </h4>
</div>
```

This code displays the Date, the *Write Comment* link, and the post category underneath the title of every post, just like in the previous **Hello World**. Notice that there are three items that are each contained within a span class: one for post-date, one for post-comments, and one for post-category.

If you delete the entire span class for the post-comments element (as highlighted in the code), you will remove the *Write Comment* link from all your posts.

 Depending upon your theme, you may also need to repeat the above instructions on the Main Index Template (index.php).

Before you leave the **Single Post** page, also look for and delete the following little snippet of code: <?php comments_template(); ?>.

Deleting this code snippet will remove any traces of *Comments Off* or *No Comments* that appear in your theme. If your theme also has a **Page Template (page.php)**, look for and delete that same bit of code there as well. By doing so, you will remove all traces of comments on any pages that you create within WordPress.

If you successfully followed these instructions, all traces of comments should now be erased from your theme.

 If you decide at any point to switch themes, you will need to repeat these steps for the newly activated theme.

Setting up a static front page

By default, the main page of your WordPress site shows a running list of your latest posts. While this is perfectly acceptable for a personal blog, an e-commerce site typically takes a more static approach so as not to confuse any first-time visitors.

Fortunately, configuring a static front page is simple. We first, need to create a new page that will become the default front page. In your WordPress Dashboard, navigate to **Pages** and select **Add New,** as shown in the following screenshot:

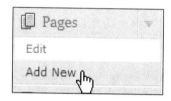

Add any variety of information that you would like first-time visitors to see, such as a logo, a welcome message, a breakdown of product categories, or whatever you would like.

When you've finished, go ahead and publish your page. The page we created for our music shop is titled *Welcome*. Now let's set it as the default front page. Back in the WordPress Dashboard, browse to **Settings** and click on the **Reading** option, as shown in the following screenshot:

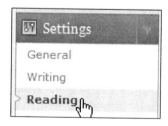

Underneath **Reading Settings**, select the option to display a static front page. Be sure to choose the title of the desired **static page** from the drop-down list. Note that we chose **Welcome**, the same page that we just added. The following screenshot shows the **Reading Settings** options:

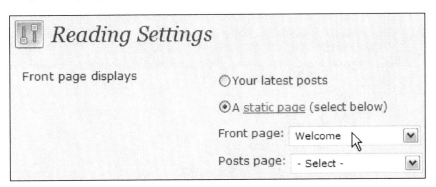

Another good option for a static front page is to directly choose the *Products Page* from the drop-down list. The *Products Page* is automatically created when you activate the e-Commerce plugin for the first time, and is essentially the gateway to your e-commerce shop. If you want customers to first see your products when they visit your site, choose this option.

Using widgets

Also known as "sidebar accessories", widgets are one of the slickest and easiest ways to vary the content of your WordPress sidebars. With widgets, you can elegantly add text, images, gadgets, HTML, or any other design elements to one or more sidebars on your site. A growing number of plugins for WordPress also come with additional widget features, including the WP e-Commerce plugin.

To get started with widgets, navigate to **Appearance** in your Dashboard and click on **Widgets,** as shown in the following screenshot:

Feast your eyes on the number of **Available Widgets**. The following screenshot shows the different widgets available:

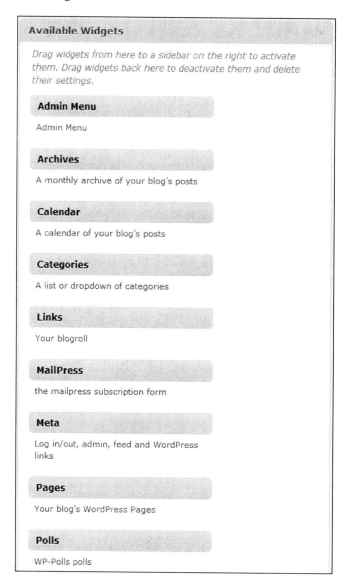

Adding a widget to your desired sidebar is a simple, click-and-drag affair. You can add as many widgets as you like to the sidebar, and re-arranging them is as easy as dragging and dropping them.

Here are the three widgets that we added to our music shop: a **Search** box, a **Text** Widget, and the **Shopping Cart**. The **Shopping Cart** widget is shown in the following screenshot:

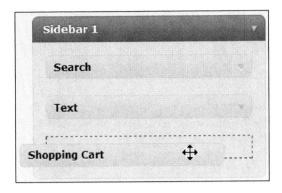

Creating text widgets

For an e-commerce site, a text widget is like a Swiss Army Knife since it's one simple tool that can serve a variety of purposes. Here are a few tasks that text widgets can accomplish:

- Create a "Featured Product" widget and rotate the contents every few days or weeks
- Add a custom image that links to a specific product category, such as "Albums" or "Singles"
- Create an HTML drop-down list with links to all product categories
- Add notices about sales or special discounts

Here's an example: let's say we want to let our customers know about a special coupon code for our shop that is valid during the month of April. A text widget is the perfect way to let all visitors know about the sale.

Drag and drop an empty text widget and place it in the sidebar. It should expand automatically, and now we can type all of the necessary text and HTML.

In the following screenshot, we've added some text and a little HTML. The **Title** of the text widget is now **April Sale!**. The <p> tags simply format the text into paragraphs, and the <strong> tag makes the coupon code show up in bold text. The usage of these tags is shown in the following screenshot:

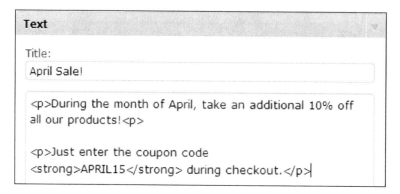

Be sure to save all of the changes once you have created the text widget. If we now take a look at the front page of our music shop, we can see the widget layout and the sale information in the WordPress sidebar, as shown in the following screenshot:

Complementary plugins

Though the WP e-Commerce plugin is the focal point of this book, there are a number of other plugins that can greatly augment the functionality of your site. They include:

- Akismet
- All in One SEO Pack
- Google XML Sitemaps
- WP-DB-Backup
- WP-Polls

Akismet

The Akismet plugin comes with WordPress by default, but if for some reason you do not have it, download it from the link `http://akismet.com/download/`. What does Akismet do? It essentially eradicates comment spam, which is a true bane to anyone running a blog with comments enabled. Granted, if you already disabled comments, your site has no need for an anti-spam plugin. For the rest of us, Akismet (or a similar plugin) is mandatory. After all, you wouldn't want your business blog flooded with rogue, distasteful comments would you?

Caught Spam

Akismet has caught **20,259 spam** for you since you first installed it.

You have no spam currently in the queue. Must be your lucky day. :)

The Akismet plugin is free for personal or hobby use. If your online store is a full-fledged commercial venture, they ask you to purchase a commercial license.

 A similar free plugin is WordPress SpamFree. For more information, refer to: `http://bit.ly/wp-spamfree`.

All in One SEO Pack

Download link: `http://bit.ly/wp-seo-pack`

The SEO pack for WordPress is designed to help your site rank higher in search engines. While the effectiveness of the SEO pack is determined by a large number of factors, especially the content of your site, using this plugin certainly doesn't hurt. Just understand that installing and activating it is not likely to rocket you to the top of Google overnight.

All in One SEO Pack specializes in allowing you to set your own titles, descriptions, and keywords, both for your site's front page and individual posts. You can see it in action in the following sample music shop screenshot:

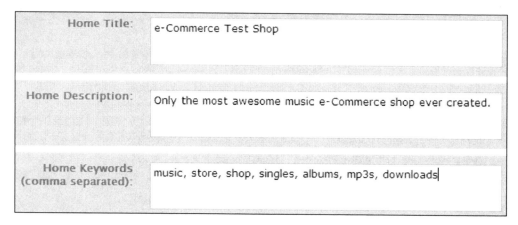

Google XML Sitemaps

Download link: `http://bit.ly/google-sitemaps`

In conjunction with the All in One SEO Pack, the Google XML Sitemaps plugin is designed to make it easier for major search engines to crawl and index your site. Activating the plugin will create a sitemap (compatible with `http://www.sitemaps.org`) that major search engines such as Ask.com, Google, MSN, and Yahoo! understand.

The following screenshot shows the Google XML Sitemaps plugin in action. Adding or updating a post will automatically rebuild the sitemap.

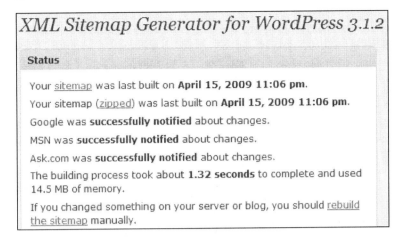

The ideal end result is that if the search engines understand and index your site in a better way, new visitors will find your store more easily.

WP-DB-Backup

Download link: `http://bit.ly/db-backup`.

WP-DB-Backup has one single purpose: it exports a backup of your WordPress database that you can restore later in case of an emergency. Upon installation, you will find a **Backup** option underneath the **Tools** menu in the Dashboard, as shown in the following screenshot:

It's better to be safe than sorry, so please don't overlook this plugin. The last thing you want is to find out that your server got hacked and you have no database backup to restore. Ouch!

WP-Polls

Download link: http://bit.ly/wp-polls

WP-Polls provide an easy way to add interactive polls to your site, either on an individual post, a page, or embedded within the sidebar via a widget. Once installed, the **Polls** menu shows up in the WordPress Dashboard.

You can create as many answers as you like for each poll, plus add automatic closing times. Since we're building a music shop, how about asking our visitors about their favorite music genre? This also directly helps us learn more about our customers. Notice the poll embedded within our WordPress sidebar in the following screenshot:

Adding a contact form

No e-commerce site is complete without providing a way for customers to contact the shop owner(s). Fortunately, this is an easy task to accomplish. Some themes for WordPress already contain a "Contact" page template. If your theme does not, there are a multitude of plugins that can bolt on that functionality with only a click or two. Here are three options:

- WordPress SpamFree contact form
- Contact Form 7
- cforms II

WordPress SpamFree contact form

Download link: `http://bit.ly/wp-spamfree`

If you opted to use the aforementioned WordPress SpamFree plugin, then rejoice! A simple, yet functional contact form is already included. To add it, first create a new page (not a post), switch to the **HTML** editing tab, and add the following tag: `<!--spamfree-contact-->`, as shown in the following screenshot:

The WordPress SpamFree contact form doesn't have many bells and whistles, but if all you need is a simple form that customers can use to contact you, it suffices nicely.

Contact Form 7

Download link: `http://bit.ly/contact-form-7`

If you require more than a single contact form on your site, consider the Contact Form 7 plugin. It supports multiple forms, basic customization via simple markup language, CAPTCHA support, and spam filtering via Akismet.

Usage is similar to the WordPress SpamFree contact form.
To add a new form, create a new page (not post) and add the following tag:
`[contact-form 1 "Contact form 1"]`.

cforms II

Download link: `http://bit.ly/cforms`

The cforms II plugin offers a plethora of configuration options for your contact form. If you need ultimate control over the customization of your form(s), cforms II will not disappoint you. A small sample of the options are included here:

- Multiple forms
- AJAX-supported form submission
- File attachment support
- Timing and submission limits
- Widget support

Adding a business blog

Up to this point, we've worked hard to convert WordPress from a traditional blogging platform into a more appropriate business platform. However, we can't deny that blogging is ultimately the strength of WordPress. Business blogging is rapidly becoming more popular. Although you can certainly create a functional e-commerce site with WordPress using nothing but static pages and the WP e-Commerce plugin, the addition of dynamic content on a blog helps give your shop a personal element. It provides the customer with a sense of the face and personality behind the store. If nothing else, it can serve as a medium for communication between you, as a store owner, and your visitors.

Adding a business blog only takes a few clicks. As we created a static front page earlier, we first need to create an empty page that will serve as the placeholder for the blog. In your WordPress Dashboard, add a new **Page**. Give it a title, such as *Blog*. You don't need to add any content to the page.

Just like when we created a static front page, navigate to **Settings** and click on **Reading**. Underneath **Reading Settings**, click on the drop-down list next to **Posts page** and choose the **Blog** page that you created. The **Reading Settings** options are shown in the following screenshot:

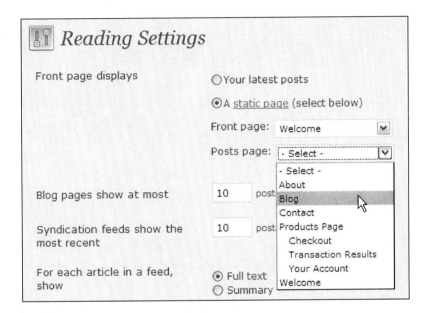

What we have just done is select a default location for all of the new posts that we will create as part of our business blog. As our site uses a static front page, it will remain the same, but all new posts will show up on the **Blog** page.

See for yourself. If you write a new post, it now appears as part of our business blog. The following screenshot shows the **Blog** page:

Summary

Congratulations! You have now completed all of the basic prerequisites needed to prepare your WordPress site for use as an e-commerce platform. In this chapter, we covered:

- Installing and activating the WP e-Commerce plugin
- How to install and activate third-party themes
- Instructions for disabling comments on posts and pages, both on an individual and a global basis
- Adding new pages and setting a static front page
- How widgets add massive flexibility and functionality to any WordPress e-commerce site
- A range of recommended, complementary third-party plugins, including tools for spam protection, search engine optimization, database backup, and polls
- Three different options for adding a contact form, ranging from simple to advanced
- Taking advantage of WordPress' strength as a blogging platform to add a business blog that allows for interaction with customers

Your store-in-progress should now look and act much more like a business platform and much less like a blog. In the next chapter, we'll begin tackling our WP e-Commerce settings.

3
Configure Your e-Commerce Settings

A smoothly running e-commerce store requires some time spent configuring the initial plugin settings. For instance, where should the shopping cart appear on your site? How much tax should buyers have to pay? What about e-mail reports?

Fortunately, most of these settings only need to be configured once, but they are integral to making your store function properly. Let's get started. All of the following options can be found by expanding the **Products** section of the WordPress Dashboard and then clicking on **Settings,** as shown in the following screenshot:

On the **Settings** page, you should see tabs across the top of the page labeled: **General**, **Presentation**, **Admin**, **Shipping**, **Payment Options**, **Import**, and **Checkout**. All settings, except for those related to payments and shipping, are addressed in this chapter.

This chapter will cover the following topics:

- General Settings
- Presentation Settings
- Admin Settings
- Checkout settings

General Settings

All of the following options are available under the **General** tab on the **Settings** page. These options include:

- Base Country/Region, Tax Settings, and Language
- Currency Settings

Base Country/Region, Tax Settings, and Language

First things first, let's configure the **Base Country/Region** of the operation. Why is this important? Choosing a Base Country/Region of operation allows the WP e-Commerce plugin to automatically handle any necessary tax calculations for you. Select a country from the **Base Country/Region** drop-down list, and if applicable, a list of regions will become available. For instance, if you select Canada as your base country, you can then choose from a list of available **Regions**.

Our sample music shop is located in **California**, so let's make the appropriate selections, as shown in the following screenshot:

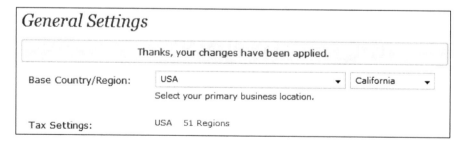

Notice that we now have some **Tax Settings** that we can configure. Naturally, **Tax Settings** vary by country and region, but for the USA, we can set sales tax rates by clicking the link for **51 Regions**. **California** has a sales tax rate of **7.25%**, so let's set it accordingly, as shown in the following screenshot:

GST/Tax Rate

Alabama: 0 %	Iowa: 0 %	New Hampshire: 0 %	Texas: 0 %
Alaska: 0 %	Kansas: 0 %	New Jersey: 0 %	Utah: 0 %
Arizona: 0 %	Kentucky: 0 %	New Mexico: 0 %	Vermont: 0 %
Arkansas: 0 %	Louisiana: 0 %	New York: 0 %	Virginia: 0 %
California: 7.25 %	Maine: 0 %	North Carolina: 0 %	Washington: 0 %
Colorado: 0 %	Maryland: 0 %	North Dakota: 0 %	Washington DC: 0 %
Connecticut: 0 %	Massachusetts: 0 %	Ohio: 0 %	West Virginia: 0 %
Delaware: 0 %	Michigan: 0 %	Oklahoma: 0 %	Wisconsin: 0 %
Florida: 0 %	Minnesota: 0 %	Oregon: 0 %	Wyoming: 0 %
Georgia: 0 %	Mississippi: 0 %	Pennsylvania: 0 %	
Hawaii: 0 %	Missouri: 0 %	Rhode Island: 0 %	
Idaho: 0 %	Montana: 0 %	South Carolina: 0 %	
Illinois: 0 %	Nebraska: 0 %	South Dakota: 0 %	
Indiana: 0 %	Nevada: 0 %	Tennessee: 0 %	

Save Changes

No matter what the country or region, any percentage you set in the **Tax Settings** will automatically be charged to the buyer during the checkout process.

Default language

Out-of-the-box, the default language for the e-Commerce plugin is **English**. As of this writing, the plugin lacks a convenient way for the customer to switch between languages, though hopefully, this is an upcoming feature.

However, you may choose an alternate language for display on your store. There are currently nineteen language files available, and whichever one you select will be the one displayed on all of your stored pages. As there is currently no easy way for customers to switch between languages, choose whichever language your customers will expect.

Currency Settings

At the bottom of the **General Settings** page are options for setting and displaying the currency type. From the drop-down list, choose the **Currency type** that your shop uses. Our music shop operates with the **US Dollar** option.

Finally, choose how you wish your store to display the numbers and symbols of your desired currency:

Once you are finished with the **General Settings**, switch to the **Presentation** tab at the top of the page.

Presentation Settings

The **Presentation** tab includes a plethora of available options for controlling how your store looks and operates. Specific categories include:

- Button Settings
- Product Settings
- Product Page Settings
- Shopping Cart Settings
- Product Group Settings
- Thumbnail Settings
- Pagination settings
- Comment Settings

Button Settings

The first set of options on this page addresses how customers interact with your products. The following screenshot shows the **Button Settings** options:

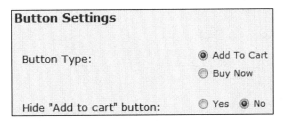

There are two options available next to **Button Type**, and the difference between the two is functional, not just aesthetic. The default option, **Add To Cart**, allows customers to add as many products as they like to the shopping cart before going through the checkout process. If you select **Buy Now** as the **Button Type**, you essentially bypass the shopping cart entirely. When customers decide to purchase a product or service, they are immediately directed to the payment processor without the need to hold items in a cart. As of this writing, the **Buy Now** option only works with PayPal and Google Checkout. Again, most people should stick with the default **Add To Cart** option, unless you know that your customers are likely to buy only one item or service at a time.

The **Hide "Add to cart" button** is set to **No** by default. Switching it to **Yes** essentially disables the entire e-commerce functionality as no customer will be able to add products to the shopping cart. Most people should keep this option set to **No**, thereby keeping the cart visible.

Product Settings

Underneath the **Button Settings** are the **Product Settings** which gives you an assortment of options with regard to how customers can interact with your products. The following screenshot shows the **Product Settings** options:

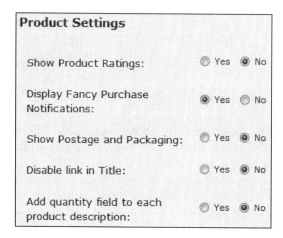

If you want your customers to be able to rate your products, set the **Show Product Ratings** option to **Yes**. Doing so will enable a five-star rating system beneath each product, which will keep track of all customer ratings. Notice the gold stars at the bottom of the **Sample CD** product shown in the following screenshot:

If you enable **Display Fancy Purchase Notifications**, users will immediately see a slick, in-line notification after they add an item to their shopping cart. The notification includes links to **Go to Checkout** and to **Continue Shopping**, as shown in the following screenshot:

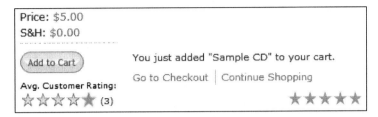

The fancy notifications provide another level of reinforcement to make sure customers know exactly where to go to check out, just in case they fail to notice that their cart has been updated.

The **Show Postage and Packaging** option, otherwise known as Shipping and Handling, displays a shipping cost below each item in your products page. When enabled, it shows up as **P&P** underneath each product in your catalog. If you disable this option, only the shipping cost is displayed on the checkout page.

You can change the default **P&P** label to anything else you please by editing the appropriate language file. To do so, launch your favorite FTP/SFTP program and browse to: `<your-WordPress-install>/wp-content/plugins/wp-e-commerce/languages/`. For English, find the file that begins with EN and open it in a text editor. Look for the line that reads:

```
define('TXT_WPSC_PNP', 'P&amp;P');.
```

For the record, its current line number is 757. This is the line that controls how the postage and packaging variable gets displayed on your site. The final part contained within the single quotes (`P&amp;P`) translates to **P&P**. Feel free to edit it however you like. To make it display **S&H** instead of **P&P**, change it to:

```
define('TXT_WPSC_PNP', 'S&amp;H');.
```

The **Disable link in Title** option does exactly what it says. It prevents the product title from displaying as a hyperlink that would normally lead to the product page with detailed information about that individual product. If you choose to disable this option, keep in mind that you may limit your customers' ability to navigate to the individual product page.

The final option under this section deals with quantity. If you enable the option to **Add quantity field to each product description,** your customers will be offered a **Quantity** box within which to specify how many of that specific product they want to buy before they click on the **Add To Cart** button. The following screenshot shows the **Format** and **Quantity** options:

Product Page Settings

The largest number of presentation options falls under the **Product Page Settings** category. The following screenshot shows the available options:

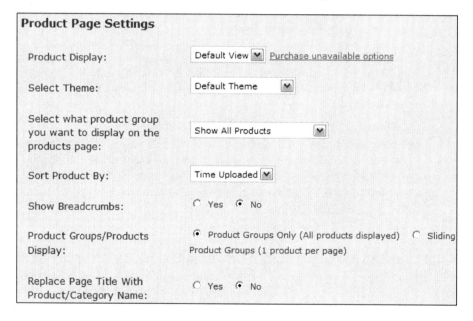

Unless you purchased any of the Gold Cart upgrades, there is only one view available next to **Product Display**. Have no fear, the Gold Cart is not required for a fully operational e-commerce site.

There are three options available next to **Select Theme**: **Default Theme**, **iShop Theme**, and **Marketplace Theme**. These options have nothing to do with your choice of theme for WordPress, but are rather for how your shopping cart is displayed. For instance, take a look at the following screenshots showing a sample product. All that changes in the three images is the theme.

Default Theme: The following screenshot shows how the default settings look with the standard **Add To Cart** button:

iShop Theme: This theme has more of a subtle look with a rounded, aqua-style **Add to Cart** button, as shown in the following screenshot:

Marketplace Theme: This theme features slightly larger text and a more-prominent ADD TO CART button, as shown in the following screenshot:

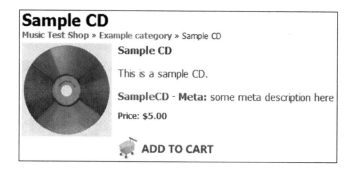

As you might guess, there is only an aesthetic difference between the three shop themes, not a functional difference. Feel free to try each of them before settling on a theme.

The drop-down list next to **Select what product group you want to display on the products page** is one of the more important settings for defining how your store will look. When customers visit your online store, they first arrive at a default products page. This products page could contain a full listing of your product catalog, or only a single product category. For example, our sample music store will sell printed sheet music, PDFs, audio CDs, and perhaps a few posters. If we wish for customers to see all of our items upon first glance, we should be sure to choose **Show All Products** from the drop-down list, as shown in the following screenshot:

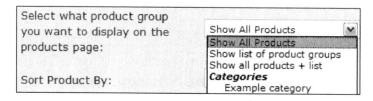

On the other hand, if we want customers to only see our printed sheet music by default, we can choose the appropriate category. Customers can view the other items by clicking on the related category link later. For now, we have not yet created our other categories, so feel free to stick with **Show All Products**. We can always change this setting after we have completed our product catalog.

The **Sort Product By** option allows for three choices: **Name, Price,** or **Time Uploaded**. Sorting is from top to bottom, therefore:

- **Name**: The option **Name** sorts your products alphabetically
- **Price**: The option **Price** sorts your products from lowest to highest price
- **Time Uploaded**: The option **Time Uploaded** sorts your products from oldest to newest

When enabled, the **Show Breadcrumbs** option simply displays a hierarchy of navigation links (colloquially known as "breadcrumbs") at the top of each individual product page. Notice that **Music Test Shop** and **Example category** are both active links in the following screenshot:

The **Product Groups/Product Display** toggle gives you a choice between displaying all of your products when a certain category is displayed, or between displaying only a single product at a time under that category. Most shop owners are likely to opt for the first option by default. However, depending on the nature and number of your products, the latter option may be right for you. When in doubt, just give it a try.

Last, but certainly not least, is an often-overlooked option to **Replace Page Title With Product/Category Name**. What does this option do? Let's take a look. If we keep this option set to **No** and click on any group name for our store (for example, **Wind Ensemble**), the breadcrumbs that we enabled will update to that group name like this: **Music Test Shop >> Wind Ensemble**. However, the heading for the page will still display as the generic **Products Page**, as shown in the following screenshot:

It looks, innocuous, right? While it isn't harmful at all, it certainly isn't very descriptive. Now, let's go back and change the **Replace Page Title With Product/Category Name** option to **Yes**. If we refresh the previous category page, the breadcrumbs will stay the same, but the page heading will be updated to the name of the group or category, as shown in the following screenshot:

Though it's a seemingly small difference, the inclusion of the category name in the page heading is more descriptive and may even provide a little boost to search engine optimization. Most users should leave this option enabled.

Shopping Cart Settings

As seen below, there are three options available with regard to the shopping cart:

* **Cart Location**
* **Use Sliding Cart**
* **Display "+ Postage & Tax"**

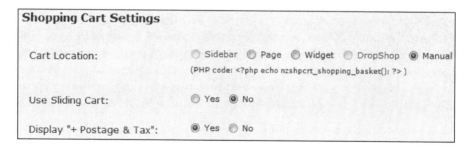

Cart Location

Unless you purchase the Gold Cart upgrades, the only available locations for placing the shopping cart are on the **Products Page**, within a widget, or manually using a snippet of PHP code.

If in doubt, stick with the **Widget** option. Choosing a location for the shopping cart is as simple as dragging and dropping a widget from the **Appearance** section of the WordPress Dashboard (for an introduction to widgets, please refer to Chapter 2, *Getting Ready to Sell*). If you choose the **Page** option, take note that this does not create a separate page dedicated to the shopping cart. Instead, it embeds the cart directly into your **Products Page,** as shown in the following screenshot:

For more advanced users, a third option is to forgo the **Widget** and **Page** elements and use a short snippet of PHP. The code is as follows:

```php
<?php echo wpsc_shopping_cart(); ?>
```

Within the PHP tags, the echo construct outputs the shopping basket information. Wherever you place that code snippet in your WordPress theme, it will reference the shopping cart. For example, you could try placing the cart in the theme header or footer.

Use Sliding Cart

When this option is enabled, the customer can choose to collapse or expand the shopping cart by clicking on the + or – button next to the cart. This is shown in two separate screenshots below.

The collapsed cart is shown in the following screenshot:

The expanded cart is shown in the following screenshot:

Display "+ Postage & Tax"

Similar to the **Show Postage and Packaging** option mentioned earlier, by enabling this option you can preemptively show customers any additional postage and tax values for their purchase(s) before they proceed to checkout, as shown in the following screenshot:

Product Group Settings

As seen below, there are a few options currently available for the Product Group Settings:

- **Show Product Group Description**
- **Show Product Group Thumbnails**
- **Show Product Count per Product Group**

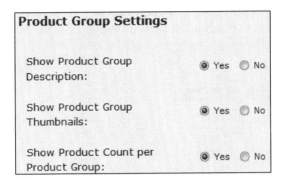

Show Product Group Description

When this option is enabled, it displays a custom description at the top of every product group page. When customers view all items in a particular group, you can choose to set a short text description for all of the items in that group. See the text in the following screenshot that reads: **Here is an example product group description**:

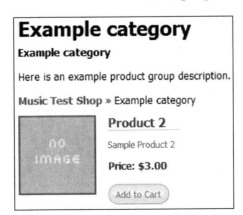

We haven't created any product groups yet, so feel free to leave this option disabled for now.

Show Product Group Thumbnails

Though entirely optional, image thumbnails can bring a spark of personality and uniqueness to your store. By enabling this option, a small custom image can be displayed that represents an entire group of items.

Show Product Count per Product Group

When enabled, this option shows a running count of products that are available per group, next to each product group link. For instance, if you are using the **Group** widget in your WordPress sidebar, all of your group names will appear in the sidebar with a number shown in brackets next to them.

Thumbnail Settings

Speaking of thumbnails, this is where we can configure their global settings. In this section, we can view and edit the default size for all of the thumbnails, depending on location. All thumbnail images are measured in pixels. The following screenshot shows the **Thumbnail Settings** options:

The default pixel values will likely work for most people, but you must make a decision here with regard to thumbnail proportion: do you want to display thumbnails that are square, wide (horizontal), or tall (vertical)? Yes, it makes a difference, so all the images of your items should have the same orientation. The default values are set to display square thumbnails, so make any proportional adjustments accordingly.

The default product thumbnail images are what customers see whenever they view a group page or your entire catalog. Users see a single product image whenever they click on a single item to view more information, provided you kept the **Hide Product Name Links** option disabled on the **General Settings** tab. Since the same image is used for both parameters, you must keep the same proportion when configuring their sizes. Yes, it is fine to use a differing size for *Default* versus *Single* images, but keep the same proportion lest you end up with elongated or squished images.

As a last resort, you can always decide that thumbnail images are too much trouble and switch the **Show Thumbnails** option to **No**.

Pagination settings

At the bottom of the **Presentation** page, we find options related to **Pagination settings**. The following screenshot shows the **Pagination settings** options:

The more products you have, the more likely you will need to enable **Pagination settings**, which enables the use of multiple pages per product group. When you click on the **Yes** option, you may enter a number for how many products you wish to display on each page.

The **Page Number position** option controls where the links for the page numbers should be displayed: at the **Top** of the page, at the **Bottom**, or **Both**. The choice is up to you, but if you have many items to display on each page, your customers will find it more convenient to have page numbers displayed at the top and bottom of every page. This means less potential scrolling and confusion.

Comment Settings

The only option here, as seen in the following screenshot is whether or not to enable the **Use IntenseDebate Comments** (http://www.intensedebate.com), which add a number of additional "social" aspects to traditional commenting systems, such as commenter profiles, reputation points, and integration with Twitter.

The majority of online stores will not require these features, but it's nice that they are available. Naturally you will need an account with IntenseDebate in order to integrate them into your shop.

Admin Settings

The **Admin** tab contains various settings related to administrative use. Specifically, you can configure settings for digital downloads, purchases, and e-mail. The **Admin Settings** are mainly used to control the following:

- Digital downloads
- Purchases
- E-mail settings
- URL Settings

The following screenshot shows the **Admin Settings** options:

Admin Settings

Max downloads per file:	1
Lock downloads to IP address:	○ Yes ◉ No
Purchase Log Email:	purchases@example-store.net
Reply Email:	support@example-store.net
Terms and Conditions:	By clicking "Submit Order", you understand that you will be transferred to a 3rd-party payment processor, such as PayPal or Google Checkout. If your order contains a digital

Digital downloads

If your e-commerce store sells any digital downloads, you have two critical options to configure: the maximum number of download attempts and whether or not to restrict downloads by IP address. The plugin completely automates the delivery of digital goods, but we need to provide some security restrictions. While we trust our customers, we want to eliminate any possibility that a customer could casually forward a download link to everyone in his address book, right?

When customers purchase any digital product on your site, they will immediately receive an encrypted download link by e-mail following payment. By default, customers only get *one attempt* to download each file that they purchase. In most cases, this is perfectly sufficient and prevents casual piracy. If you wish to relax this restriction, simply increase the number next to **Max downloads per file**.

As an additional security measure, you can choose to **Lock downloads to IP address**. This is another security precaution designed to thwart casual piracy. When enabled, the e-commerce plugin takes note of the IP address for the computer that was used to make the purchase. Once the customer clicks on the download link that she receives, the IP address for the computer requesting the download is checked against the originating IP address for the purchase. If the plugin finds a match, it allows the download to proceed. If not, the download is blocked.

Though this security precaution sounds great, it can lead to numerous problems in reality. Imagine this scenario: Jane makes a purchase from your store at the end of her workday at the office. When she gets home, she checks her e-mail and finds the download link for your product. Guess what happens when she clicks on the link? Jane's download is blocked because the originating computer is now different. She is not likely to be very understanding when she sends you an angry e-mail.

While Jane's situation may be rare, it can happen. It's up to you to think critically about how you want to handle the security of your digital downloads. One important aspect to keep in mind is that if you do encounter the situation in which customers are legitimately blocked from accessing downloads, you can easily unlock them. Just check your sales records for the details on that transaction.

Purchases

If you want the e-commerce plugin to notify you by e-mail whenever someone makes a purchase, enter an e-mail address in the blank field next to **Purchase Log Email**. You may enter more than one e-mail address here, separated by commas. This is useful if you have one or more partners helping you run the store.

The **Purchase Log Email** option is useful, but there is no guarantee that a customer has actually completed a transaction. In its current form, the plugin dispatches the purchase log e-mails once the customer is sent from your site to the selected third-party payment processor (such as PayPal or Google Checkout). This process is greatly simplified if you use PayPal IPN (see Chapter 6, *Checkout and Payment Setup*). Be sure to verify that the transaction has actually completed if you decide not to use PayPal IPN.

The **Reply Email** field contains the e-mail address that customers can use as their contact whenever they reply to any e-mail message sent directly from your store. Any content that you put in the **Terms and Conditions** box is likely to be the last thing that customers read before making their purchase. The link to the **Terms and Conditions** is shown in the following screenshot:

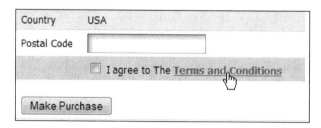

As you might suspect, customers must agree to the **Terms and Conditions** that you set before they can continue with the purchase. Some useful information provided in it could include clarification that they are about to proceed to a third-party payment processor, your refund policy, or general information about digital downloads. The content that you write can be styled with HTML. The following is a sample to get you started:

```
<p>By clicking <em>Submit Order<em>, you understand that you will be
transferred to a 3rd-party payment processor, such as PayPal or Google
Checkout.</p>

<p>If your order contains a digital download, you understand that
you will receive an e-mail with a link where you can download the
purchased product. You will NOT receive a shipment in the mail for any
digital product purchases.</p>

<p><strong>Refund Policy:</strong> No refunds will be given for the
purchase of digital content.</p>
```

The brief set of **Terms and Conditions** in the previous code uses paragraph tags to put space between paragraphs, and uses a little bit of bold and italics for emphasis. When a customer views it, it will look like the following screenshot:

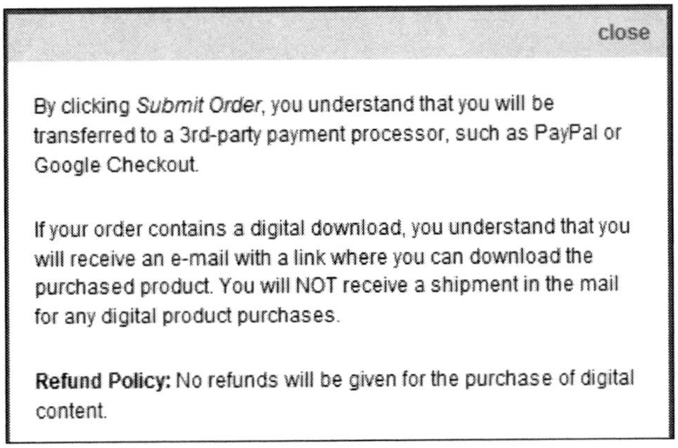

E-mail settings

Whenever you make a purchase with a big retailer such as Amazon, what is the first thing that happens? You soon receive an e-mail from the retailer thanking you for your business and providing details about your recent order, correct? That kind of feedback is comforting to customers, and that's exactly what we are about to configure now.

In the box next to **Purchase Receipt**, any content that you enter is what the customer will receive immediately after completing a purchase. Take your time with this information since it is the primary means by which you will communicate with your customers. Unlike the **Terms and Conditions** message, avoid any HTML here because it may not be interpreted by the customer's e-mail client.

Instead of using HTML, you may use a number of tags for including variables such as the total price, items ordered, and order number. Some of the tags are as follows:

- **%shop_name%**: This tag includes the name of your store as specified in your WordPress **General Settings**
- **%product_list%**: This tag includes a list of all purchased items
- **%total_price%**: This tag displays the total amount charged, including shipping
- **%total_shipping%**: This tag indicates only the amount charged for shipping

Let's view a sample **Purchase Receipt** in action. First, an initial configuration:

```
Thank you for purchasing with %shop_name%. Any items to be shipped
will be processed as soon as possible. Shipping usually takes 5-7
business days. If your purchase includes any digital products, you
will find download links below.

All prices include tax plus shipping and handling where applicable.

Your order includes these items:

%product_list%

%total_shipping%

%total_price%
```

Notice that we called every possible variable using all of the tags. This information will appear directly in the website immediately following a purchase, and it will also be sent to the customer specified e-mail address. The following screenshot shows how it might look as part of a live transaction:

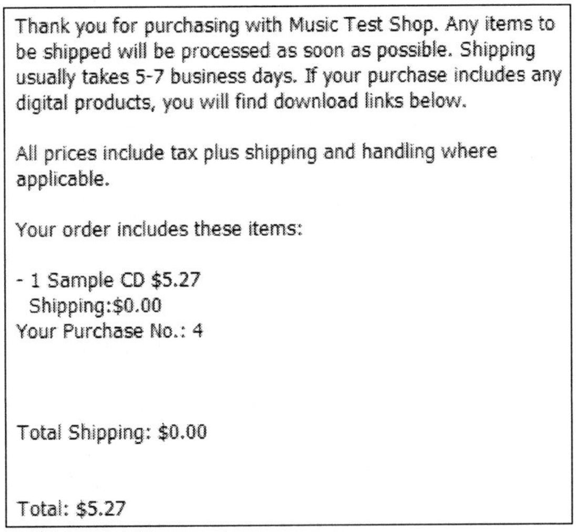

Thank you for purchasing with Music Test Shop. Any items to be shipped will be processed as soon as possible. Shipping usually takes 5-7 business days. If your purchase includes any digital products, you will find download links below.

All prices include tax plus shipping and handling where applicable.

Your order includes these items:

- 1 Sample CD $5.27
  Shipping:$0.00
Your Purchase No.: 4

Total Shipping: $0.00

Total: $5.27

The **Admin Report** is a scaled-down version of the purchase receipt. Any information that you provide in this box will be sent to the address that you specified earlier in the **Purchase Log Email** field.

As the **Admin Report** is mainly for just informative and archival purposes, specifying a few tags is sufficient. The following screenshot shows some of the tags used in the **Admin Report**:

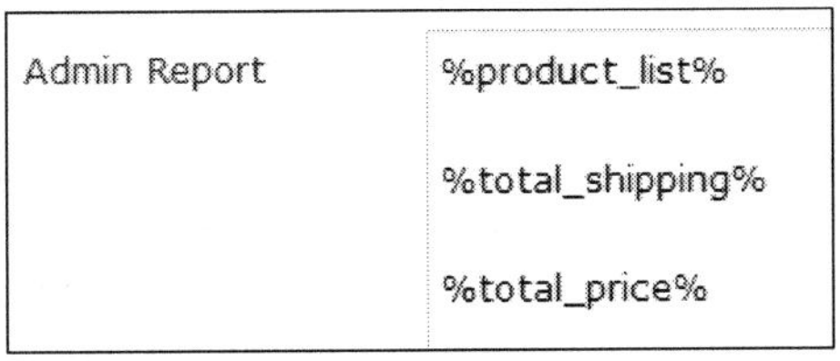

Admin Report	%product_list%
	%total_shipping%
	%total_price%

URL Settings

Ideally, you should never need to touch the **URL Settings**, as they are simply reflections of your WordPress permalink structure for the pages that comprise your store. The **URL Settings** are shown in the following screenshot:

URL Settings:	
The location of the product list:	http://www.example-store.net/shop/?page_
The location of the shopping cart:	http://www.example-store.net/shop/?page_
Transaction Details URL:	http://www.example-store.net/shop/?page_
User Account URL:	http://www.example-store.net/shop/?page_
	Update Page URLs | Fix Product Group Permalinks

The main scenario in which you should manipulate the **URL Settings** is if you change your **Permalinks** layout in the WordPress **Settings**. If you do so, you may find that your store suddenly disappears behind a **404 Not Found error**. To fix it, navigate to the **URL Settings** and click on the links to **Update Page URLs** and **Fix Product Group Permalinks**. Sure, this may seem inconvenient, but it boils down to a limitation to what the e-Commerce plugin authors can do as developers. Otherwise these settings would be completely automated. That said, if your store links don't seem to be working properly for some reason, try updating your **URL Settings** first.

Checkout settings

The **Checkout Options** control how much information the customer provides to you during the checkout process. The first decision you must make is whether customers are required to register as users on your site before they are allowed to check out. It's a personal decision, but many customers may be annoyed by mandatory registration. If in doubt, leave the mandatory registration disabled.

Otherwise, feel free to customize the form(s) at will. The main items to manipulate are the numerical order and whether or not certain fields are **Mandatory**.

The following screenshot shows the options available for customizing the forms:

Name	Type	Mandatory	Display in Log	Order	
1. Your billing/contact	Heading ▼	☐	☐	1	🗑
First Name	Text ▼	☑	☑	2	🗑
Last Name	Text ▼	☑	☑	3	🗑
Address	Address ▼	☑	☐	4	🗑
City	City ▼	☑	☐	5	🗑
Country	Country ▼	☑	☐	7	🗑
Postal Code	Text ▼	☑	☑	8	🗑
Phone	Text ▼	☑	☐	9	🗑

Summary

All finished? Fantastic! The majority of the settings for your e-commerce store are now configured. Thankfully, most of these items must only be addressed once, though you are welcome to revisit them at any time to continue tweaking and testing. In this chapter, we covered:

- **General Settings**—settings including those related to country, taxes, language, and currency
- **Presentation Settings**—settings specifically related to the look-and-feel of the store, including the shopping cart placement, navigation, thumbnails, and pagination
- **Admin Settings**—settings used to control the security over digital downloads, as well as purchase information and e-mail settings
- **Checkout settings**—settings used to control how much information customers must enter during the checkout process and whether or not they must register on the site before placing an order

We are now ready to build our product catalog.

Managing Your Product Catalog

Up to this point, we have focused on configuring the settings for WordPress and the e-Commerce plugin. It's now time to dig into the real meat-and-potatoes of any online store: building a catalog of products to sell.

Adding new products to the catalog is a fairly straightforward process, but there are still a number of options to consider. For instance, how does a T-shirt seller account for different sizes and colors? What about selling a digital versus a physical item? For someone with a large number of items, what elements are available to help organize and categorize them?

In this chapter, we will start building a product catalog for our music shop that sells sheet music in both physical and digital formats.

This chapter will cover the following points:

- Creating new products
- Groups, categories, and tags
- Price and Stock Control
- Variations
- Advanced Options

Creating new products

To start adding new products, we first need to navigate to the page that lists our products. In your WordPress Dashboard, expand the **Products** section and click on the **Products** link, as shown in the following screenshot:

The resulting page lists all of your existing products on the left-hand side, and all of the product details on the right-hand side. Let's add some new products. First, we'll create a physical, shippable item, and then we'll create a digital item that customers can download after purchase.

Creating a new physical product

By *physical product*, we are referring to any item that is tangible and can be shipped, such as an article of clothing, a book, or a compact disc. For our sheet music shop, most of the physical products that we will sell are in the form of printed music scores. A myriad of options are available when creating a new product. However, the only requirements for listing a new item are a **Product Name**, a **Price**, and a connection to a specific category.

With these minimal requirements in mind, let's create a new physical product. The first item that we will list is the music score for a string quartet. Under the **Add Product** section on the right-hand side of the Products page, enter the name and a price for the item. Though not required, any details that you enter in the description box below the **Price** option will appear beside the item for customers to see. The following screenshot shows the **Add Product** section:

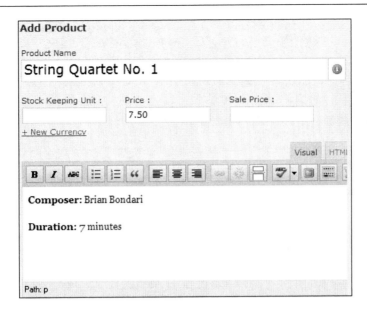

The final requirement to get your new product to appear in your store is to associate it with a category.

 Without a connection to a category, the item will show up in your WordPress Product page but will not appear in your online store for customers to buy.

If you want customers to see your products, it is imperative that you link each item to a category. The WP e-Commerce plugin creates a couple of sample categories for you. For now, simply select the checkbox next to **Example category**, and then click on the **Add Product** button at the bottom of the page. The **Categories and Tags** section is shown in the following screenshot:

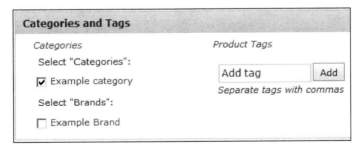

Once you have added your product, you should see it on the left-hand side of the **Display Products** page. The following screenshot shows the **String Quartet No. 1** that we created:

If you visit your online store, you should now see your first new product listing. Of course, it's rather sparse at the moment, but we will fix that shortly.

Before we move on, we should mention the **Sale Price** field, which is handy for creating temporary discounts on items. By adding a value to this field, you can specify a temporary price for that item. Customers will see a notice that the item is on sale, and the original price will appear with a strikethrough.

For instance, let's enable the **Sale Price** for the **String Quartet No. 1** that we just created. The **Sale Price** has a value of **$6.25** versus the original **$7.50**. The following screenshot shows what customers will see:

Creating a new digital product

Our sheet music shop also sells PDFs. Therefore, we need to create some products that customers can purchase and then download directly. The process is largely the same as creating a physical product, but with a couple of additional steps.

As with a physical product, the minimal information required is a **Product Name**, a **Price**, and a connection to a category. You must also have a digital file to sell, such as an MP3 or a PDF file. In our case, we're going to create a listing for the sheet music to *Ave Maria* in PDF format.

Just like before, create a new product on the **Display Products** page and give it a **Product Name** and **Price**. Any additional description is nice, but optional. Also, be sure to choose a category for your item so it will appear in your online store. The following screenshot shows the **Add Product** section for a new digital product:

To distinguish a digital product from a physical one, there are two additional steps that you need to perform. First, scroll down to the **Shipping Details** section and select the checkbox next to **Disregard Shipping for this product**. The following screenshot shows the **Shipping Details** section:

Secondly, we need to associate a file with the item listing. This is the file that customers will download after they purchase the item. In our case, customers will buy a PDF of sheet music, so we must associate the appropriate PDF with this listing.

At the bottom of the page you will find a **Product Download** section. Here, you can click on the **Browse** button to find and upload the file you want associated with this product. It's now time to add the PDF for our Ave Maria sheet music, as shown in the following screenshot:

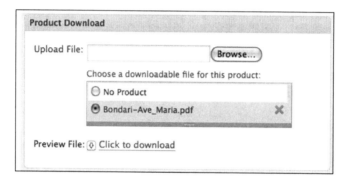

Once your file is uploaded, click on the **Preview File** link to test your download. You can also disassociate a previously uploaded file by clicking on the red **X** to the right-hand side of the existing file.

Depending on your web host, your maximum file upload size might be quite small, such as 2 Megabytes. This setting is handled by the php.ini file on your hosting package. This file might also be called php5.ini. If the limitation is acting as a constraint, consult your host's documentation (or contact them directly) for the procedure to increase your maximum file upload size.

Click on the **Add Product** button at the bottom of the page when you have finished these steps. As before, visit the front page of your online store to make sure your new product is visible.

These are the essential pieces of information you need to start listing physical and digital products. Let's now dig into some more options with regard to organization and aesthetics.

Groups, categories, and tags

A few powerful and flexible tools exist to help organize your product catalog. The main tools at your disposal are groups, categories, and tags.

Groups and categories

Creating *groups* and *categories* is one of the easiest ways to organize your products. The more products you have, the more benefit you will receive by organizing them into multiple groups. What do groups do? They allow your customers to easily sort and navigate your products. To set up your product groups, click on the **Categories** link under **Products** in your WordPress Dashboard, as shown in the following screenshot:

 Groups and categories are often confused. In prior versions of the WP e-Commerce plugin, groups were known as *categories* and *brands*. Since then, they have merged into a single unit known as groups, hopefully simplifying matters. Try thinking of groups as collections of categories and sub-categories in which the group is the master or parent category.

You can create multiple categories and sub-categories within a group, thus creating a hierarchical organization. For a clothing vendor, one common way to use groups is to create a new group called *Clothing* and a number of categories within it for *T-shirts*, *Pants*, *Shorts*, *Hats*, and more. The following figure shows how the resulting hierarchy would look:

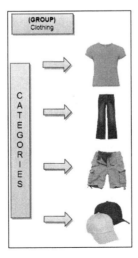

By no means are you limited to a single group. The same clothing vendor could also create another group called *Brands* and list all of his available clothing brands (e.g., *Nike* and *Converse*) as categories within that group. Customers could then easily sort products by type of clothing or brand.

For our music shop, overall we will create two groups: one for music *Genre* and the other for *Composer* name.

On the **Categories** page, the first thing we will do is click on the **Add New Group** button. As seen in the following screenshot, there are fields available for the group **Name** and an optional **Description**:

Once we have created both the groups, we can start adding categories and sub-categories within those groups. To do so, first be sure to select the appropriate group from the drop-down list. The following screenshot shows the different categories available:

We're now ready to start adding categories to our **Genre** group. Specifically, let's add categories for *Chamber*, *Choral*, *Orchestral*, and *Wind Ensemble* genres. Use the editing options on the right-hand side of the page to fill in all of the pertinent information for your category. The following screenshot shows the editing options for the different items created:

You are editing an item in the "Genre" Group

You are editing the "Chamber" Group

+ Add new category to the current Group

Display Category Shortcode:
[wpsc_products category_url_name='chamber']

Display Category Template Tag:
<?php echo wpsc_display_products(array('category_url_name'=>'chamber')); ?>

Name:
> Chamber

Description:
> Instrumental music in solo and small groups.

Group Parent:
> Select Parent

Group Image:
> [Browse...]

> Height: 96 Width: 96

> *Note: if this is blank, the image will not be resized*
> *You can upload thumbnail images for each group. To display Group details in your shop you must configure these settings under Presentation Settings.*

Delete Image:

Target Market Restrictions

Target Markets:
> Select: All None
> ☐ Afghanistan
> ☐ Albania
> ☐ Algeria
> ☐ American Samoa
> ☐ Andorra
> ☐ Angola
> ☐ Anguilla
> ☐ Antarctica

> *Select the markets you are selling this category to.*

Presentation Settings
To over-ride the presentation settings for this group you can enter in your prefered settings here

Catalog View:
> Please select

Thumbnail Size:
> Height: Width:

[**Edit Group**] Delete

Add as many categories as you need. At a minimum, you only need a product **Name**. The **Description** field is optional, but you can choose to use it to display the description about the category to your customers.

 If you want the product **Description** to also display any category description to customers, be sure to enable that option in your e-Commerce **Settings | Presentation | Product Group Settings**.

To add a sub-category, simply choose an existing category as a **Group Parent**. If you have any images you would like to set as thumbnails for each category, you can add them using the **Group Image** option. Images are optional, but can help your categories look more aesthetically pleasing.

The following screenshot shows how our completed **Genre group** looks for our music shop with images and a sub-category:

Deleting categories and groups

If you want to delete an existing category, such as the **Example Category** installed by default, first click on the **Edit** button next to appropriate category. Once the details of the category load on the right-hand side of the page, look for the **Delete** button near the bottom of the page. The **Delete** option is seen in the following screenshot:

If you want to delete an entire group, select the desired group from the drop-down list, and then click on the **Edit** link next to the group name, as shown in the following screenshot:

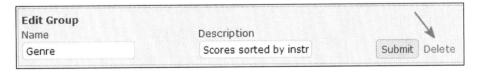

The **Name** and **Description** fields will once again load for that group. Look for the **Delete** button to the right-hand side of those fields, as shown in the following screenshot:

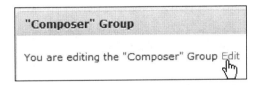

 As of this writing, you cannot delete the default group called **Categories**. However, you can rename it and use it however you would like.

Product Categories widget

As discussed in Chapter 2, *Getting Ready to Sell*, widgets are a handy way to add content or functionality to your site. With regard to groups, the WP e-Commerce plugin includes a custom widget designed to display your product groups in a WordPress sidebar. While it is not required for a functional store, it does contain some options for displaying your groups, so it's worth your consideration.

To add the widget, navigate to **Appearance | Widgets** in your WordPress Dashboard, scroll down to the **Product Categories** widget, and drag-and-drop it to your desired sidebar. The **Product Categories** widget is shown in the following screenshot:

The widget will automatically expand once you add it to your sidebar. The following screenshot shows a few options that are available:

Select each checkbox next to the groups that you wish to display. If you leave the **Title** field blank, it will display as **Product Categories** in your sidebar. Otherwise, fill in the title you entered, such as **Catalog** or **Categories**.

If you added your own images as thumbnails when you created your groups, try selecting the checkbox to display them. Be sure to click on **Save** when you are finished. Then, feast your eyes on your online store. Do you like what you see?

At this point, you have harnessed the power and flexibility of groups and categories. Use them to your advantage when you add new products or edit existing ones.

Tags

Tags are yet another organizational tool that you can use to help customers search and sort your products. By tagging your products with one or more labels, you can create a "tag cloud" that gives customers a visual indicator of how many products are associated with that particular label.

Not every store has the need for a "tag cloud", but here is an example of how it could work. For our music store, we have already created groups for **Genre** and **Composer**. We could also create tag labels for *sacred* versus *secular* music, or perhaps labels for *duos*, *trios*, and *quartets*.

You can add tags back on the Products page. While adding or editing a product, look for the **Product Tags** field as part of the **Categories and Tags** section. To add multiple labels, just add commas between them. The following screenshot shows the **Product Tags** option:

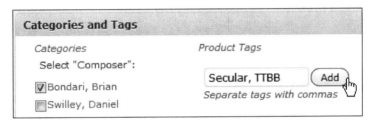

For tags to show up on your store, be sure to add the **Product Tags** widget to your sidebar. Note that this differs from the **Tag Cloud** widget that WordPress uses to display tags associated with **Posts**. The following screenshot shows the **Product Tags** widget:

When enabled, the **Product Tags** widget will display a cloud of tags you created on your store. Larger tags indicate more frequently used labels. The following figure shows an example as part of our sheet music shop:

Price and Stock Control

Back on the **Products** page, there are several options listed under **Price and Stock Control** for each product that you create. Many of them are self-explanatory, but a couple of them deserve extra discussion. The following screenshot shows the different **Price and Stock Control** options:

> **Price and Stock Control**
>
> ☐ Do not include tax (tax is set in shop config)
>
> ☐ This is a donation (only show it in the donations widget)
>
> ☐ Table Rate Price
>
> ☐ Custom Tax Rate
>
> ☐ I have a limited number of this item in stock. If the stock runs out, this product will not be available on the shop unless you untick this box or add more stock.

Specifically, the **Table Rate Price** option is handy for providing customers with a volume discount. Table Rate pricing works by providing an automatic discount when customers purchase an item in bulk. Let's say that an item ordinarily costs $3, but if a customer orders **10** or more, the price for each item drops to **$2.50**. You can add also multiple tiers to the rate. The following screenshot shows the **Table Rate Price** option:

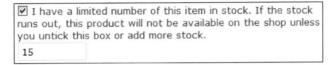

Price and Stock Control

☐ Do not include tax (tax is set in <u>shop config</u>)

☐ This is a donation (only show it in the donations widget)

☑ Table Rate Price

+ Add level

Quantity		Price
10	and above	2.50
20	and above	2.25
30	and above	2.00

If you have a limited amount of stock for a certain item, you can prevent yourself from overselling by enabling the "limited stock" option. Simply select the checkbox for this option to specify the quantity of that item you have, as shown in the following screenshot:

☑ I have a limited number of this item in stock. If the stock runs out, this product will not be available on the shop unless you untick this box or add more stock.

15

The WP e-Commerce plugin will automatically keep track of your dwindling supply, disabling customers from purchasing more of them when your stock is empty.

Variations

The **Variations** feature is a lifesaver for certain types of store-owners. What is a variation? It's a subtle difference within a single product. One common example is with regard to clothing. Picture this: James wants to create a store to sell T-shirts. Once he starts building his product catalog, he realizes that he needs a way for customers to specify what size shirt they want. He shudders to think that he might need to create a separate product listing for each size of each shirt. Not only would that be extremely time-consuming, it would be confusing for potential customers. Isn't there an easier way?

Yes! Variations are exactly what James needs. By creating a variation for size, he can create one listing for each shirt and have customers simply choose a size from a drop-down list. As an added benefit, if he needs to charge extra for an irregular size, variations can handle that as well.

Other examples of variations could be color, or perhaps whether a given product is in physical or digital format. For instance, someone selling software could create a variation allowing customers to choose between purchasing a CD or a direct download. The possibilities are endless.

As our sheet music shop sells music scores in both printed and PDF formats, this is a great opportunity to simplify our lives with a variation. We can create a variation for *print* versus *PDF*, thus removing the need to create two listings for each product. Also, as the digital downloads require less overhead for our business, we can charge less for the PDF option. Everyone wins.

To get started with creating product variations, first navigate to **Variations** under the **Products** section, as shown in the following screenshot:

Add a new variation set, giving it a **Name** of your choice, such as *Size* or *Color*. In our case, as we're talking about **Print** versus **PDF**, we are going to call it **Format**. The data fields of the **Add Variation Set** section are shown in the following screenshot:

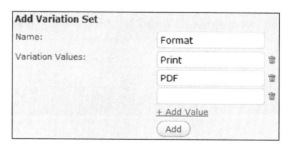

Add any values that you need and click on the **Add** button at the bottom.

> If you require more than two values, click on the **+ Add Value** button. To delete values, click on the trash can icon to the right-hand side of each value.

To see your new variation in action, return to your **Products** page and add or edit a product. You should see the name of your variation within the **Variation Control** section, as shown in the following screenshot:

Here, you can set different prices for each variation, if necessary. You can also expand each variation (as seen in the previous screenshot) by clicking on the **More** button. Additional settings include the ability to specify different weights for each variation, plus the ability to link a variation to a digital download. This is perfect for our music shop as we can link the **PDF** variation to an uploaded file, yet specify a shipping weight for our **Print** variation.

Keep in mind that you are not limited to only one variation set. You could create variations for size and color if you want.

Advanced Options

There are a number of **Advanced Options** near the bottom of each product listing. It's unlikely that you will need to adjust these options very frequently as they are tailored mainly for specific uses. The **Advanced Options** section is shown in the following screenshot:

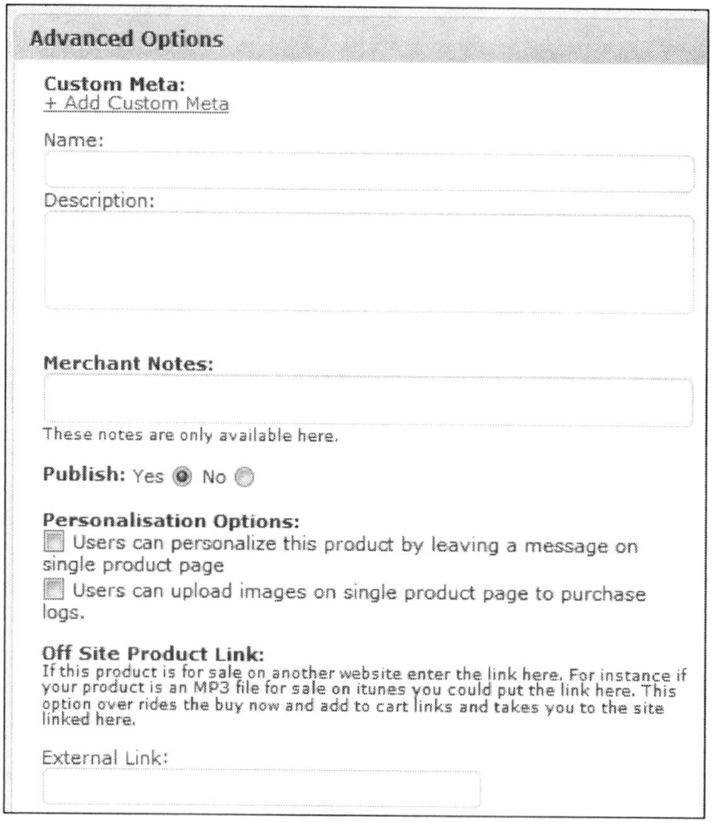

Custom Meta

If the sound of **Custom Meta** leaves you scratching your head, fear not. You can have a perfectly functioning store without ever worrying about **Custom Meta**. However, it does have some handy uses, though admittedly, you will benefit most from adding **Custom Meta** if you have upgraded to the Gold Cart module.

Most of the benefits of **Custom Meta** are related to searching. For example, if you sell movies, you most likely already have groups and categories set up for movie genres (action, comedy, and so on). What happens, though, if a customer queries a search for a particular movie director? Will he find relevant films? If you have added the film director's name to the details of your products, then perhaps he will.

However, you can make your movies easier to find by allowing your customers to search for film directors as part of your **Custom Meta**. Simply set a **Custom Meta Name**, such as *Director,* and a meta **Description** with a value containing the appropriate film director's name, such as *George Lucas* or *Steven Spielberg*. That information will appear with the product listing and is also easy to find in a search.

> The default WordPress search box only searches your posts and pages. It does not search the products you create with the WP e-Commerce plugin. Unfortunately, this is a purposeful limitation of the plugin. Purchasing the Gold Cart upgrade enables product search.

Merchant Notes

The **Merchant Notes** section is essentially just a scratchpad for jotting down any information about a particular product that you do not want anyone else to see. You can use it to save reminders about products or any other details that need to be for your eyes only.

Personalisation Options

There are two different options for personalization available to a customer. If you enable the first option, you give customers an opportunity to write some text that you can then apply to an item before shipping it. If you sell jewellery or other easily customizable items, your customers may appreciate the opportunity to add a custom message to be engraved or printed.

The second option is similar, but involves images instead of text. If this option is enabled, you can allow customers to upload a custom image that you will find in their purchase logs. If you sell custom T-shirts or other apparel, you may find this option appealing.

Summary

By now, you should have a solid start in building your e-commerce product catalog. We have created products, organized them into groups and categories, labeled them with tags, customized them with variations, and considered some personalization and advanced options. Get busy filling out the rest of the catalog. Your customers are waiting.

In this chapter, we covered:

- Creating new products — the essentials of listing both physical and digital items
- Groups, categories, and tags — the main tools at your disposal for product organization
- Price and Stock Control — the flexibility in creating special discounts, plus the ability to automatically track a limited number of items
- Variations — the power to easily manage slight differences within a single product
- Advanced Options — including those related to custom meta and customer personalization

The next chapter will continue the building process for our store as we consider user accounts for customers and staff.

5

User Accounts: Customers and Staff

WordPress is inherently a multiuser platform. Each user has a role to play, and each role is defined by its capabilities. While the use of multiple accounts is obvious for an online store with more than one partner or staff member, even a sole proprietor must contend with multiple user accounts if he allows his customers to create their own logins.

Every shop owner, whether or not he has additional partners or staff, must decide whether to allow customers to register for their own accounts or not. If the answer is *yes*, there are a few additional issues to consider and configure. For instance, should registration remain optional, or should customers be required to log in before making purchases? If there are additional staff members for the store, what permissions should they have?

In this chapter, we will explore the various roles that users can have within WordPress, and discuss how to handle customer registration, from the point of view of both a site owner as well as a customer.

This chapter covers:

- Enabling user registrations
- Understanding WordPress roles
- Staff accounts
- Customer accounts
- Creating a test customer account

Enabling user registrations

Before we delve into the various roles within WordPress, answer the following two questions:

- Do you have partners or staff who help you run your store?
- Do you want to give customers the option to create a login for your store?

If you answered *Yes* to either of the questions above, you should ensure that registration is enabled within your WordPress site. If you answered *No* to both questions, you have no need for multiple user accounts or user registration and can safely skip the rest of this chapter.

To enable user registration, navigate to **Settings | General** within your WordPress Dashboard:

About halfway down the page, look for the **Membership** section and ensure that the checkbox next to **Anyone can register** is selected:

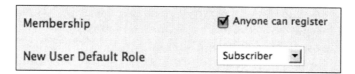

Also note that there is a drop-down menu next to **New User Default Role**. Whenever someone registers for a new account within WordPress, they will inherit the permissions and capabilities defined by the selected role. The default option is **Subscriber**, the most limited role. Unless you absolutely know that you want new accounts to have elevated privileges, such as the ability to write new posts, the default option of **Subscriber** is fine.

Understanding WordPress roles

Beginning with WordPress 2.0+, every user created under WordPress is assigned a *role*, and each role controls a varying number of predefined privileges. In WordPress lingo, these privileges are called *capabilities*. There are over forty existing capabilities in a default WordPress installation.

One of the most basic capabilities is *read*: the ability to read posts and pages. Every single role within WordPress has the *read* capability. As you might imagine, certain capabilities are more elevated than others. For instance, the ability for a user to delete his own posts (*delete_posts*) requires higher elevation than simply reading them, whereas the ability to delete posts written by other users (*delete_other_posts*) requires an even higher level of role elevation.

Every WordPress installation comes with five roles: Administrator, Editor, Author, Contributor, and Subscriber. Try not to think of one role as necessarily outranking another. Instead, each specific role contains a set of capabilities that control exactly what that user can and cannot do within the site.

Administrator

Naturally, the *Administrator* has access to all of the capabilities within WordPress, including control over themes, plugins, and other administrative settings. The first account created upon a fresh WordPress install has administrator rights, though one can always have more than one administrator account.

In addition to managing the look and feel of a site, users with administrator roles are responsible for system backups and general security.

Editor

Compared to the Administrator, users with their roles set to *Editor* have a slightly reduced set of capabilities. They have full control over all posts and pages on the site, even those written by other users, but have no access to themes, plugins, and other administrative settings.

Editor is the minimum role required to access the WP e-Commerce plugin settings.

Author

The role of *Author* continues the reduction in capabilities compared to Administrator and Editor. Users with this role can create and delete their own posts, but have neither access to posts written by other users, nor to any of the WordPress pages. *Authors* do not have sufficient privileges to access any parts of the WP e-Commerce plugin.

Contributor

Contributors only have access to a handful of WordPress capabilities. Specifically, they can edit their own posts and can create new ones, but can neither actually publish them, nor delete them once they are published. They also cannot upload any files.

New posts written by contributors must be submitted for review by an Editor or an Administrator.

Subscriber

And here we have the most basic role containing the fewest capabilities. In fact, users with *Subscriber* roles can only read posts on the site and have a limited Dashboard that contains access to only their own profile plus a few Dashboard widgets.

If customers are allowed to create accounts, their roles should automatically default to *Subscriber*.

Staff accounts

What roles, then, should you assign to other people who work for your company? Of course, that depends on what responsibilities they have. If you have an equal partner who will share all website duties, creating an additional Administrator account is the way to go. If a staff member is helping list e-commerce products, but is not assisting with design or plugins, the role of Editor is perfect. If a user only helps with writing other parts of the site, such as a business blog, the roles of Contributor or Author should work fine.

 Remember that in order for other users to assist with any aspect of the WP e-Commerce plugin, such as listing products, that user *must* have a role of **Editor** or higher.

No matter which roles you wish to assign to your users, we first need to add those users to WordPress.

Creating staff users

There are two methods of adding staff users:

1. Manual registration
2. Self-registration

Manual registration

The first method is to simply add users manually, which must be done from an account with administrative capabilities. To do so, navigate to **Users | Add New** in your WordPress Dashboard:

Once the **Add New User** page loads, you can enter all of the pertinent details for your staff member. As an example, let's add the user **John** who will assist with product listings:

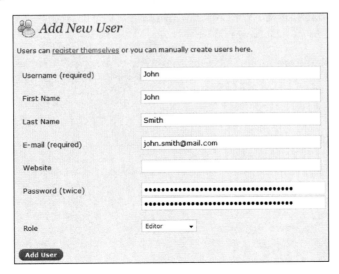

There are a couple of elements to take note of here. First of all, notice that we can go ahead and choose a **Role** for the user. Secondly, we must also set a password for that user. By now you have likely heard how important it is to create *strong* passwords. We won't belabor the point much here, but just think what could happen if an unauthorized person gains access to John's **Editor** account because of a weak password. All our posts and products could be deleted.

Since we created John's account manually, we must not forget to tell him the correct password. He can always change it himself after his first login.

Self-registration

You can also choose to let staff members register for accounts themselves. Self-registration is a snap, and there are two easy ways in which it can work. The first is to simply add the **Meta** widget to your WordPress sidebar, which will display a **Register** and **Log in** link on your site:

Another way is to e-mail a registration link to your co-workers. The self-registration link takes the form of the full URL to your WordPress installation plus the `wp-register.php` file. Provided registration is enabled and WordPress is installed in the root of your domain, the URL would look like this: `http://your-domain.com/wp-register.php`.

Either way, when staff members choose to register for an account, they will see a registration screen. The only required information is a **Username** and a valid **E-mail** address:

Upon registration, your staff members will receive an automatically generated password, which they can change upon logging in to the site. Remember that all new user accounts are set to *Subscriber* by default. Once you have confirmed a successful login, you can edit their user account to manually elevate their role.

Customer accounts

At this point, you must make a crucial decision about how you would like customers to interact with your site. Do customers need to register for an account before they are allowed to make purchases? As with most issues in life, there are positives and negatives about each viewpoint.

One strong argument for mandatory customer registration is that it opens up an order history, which all customers can see once they are logged in with their accounts. Another benefit for you, as the store owner, is that mandatory registration provides a customer catalog of sorts for you to peruse. This allows you to quickly spot repeat customers and provides a convenient place to find contact information.

One argument against mandatory registration is that it adds a potentially irritating step to the checkout process for your customers. This is easy to understand from the customer's point of view. How many times have you found an item online that you wanted to buy, only to have a forced site registration sprung upon you? Was it discouraging?

Ultimately, the decision is yours to make. One suggestion is to make customer registration optional. Those who wish to register may do so, while others are spared the inconvenience.

No matter what you decide, the place to set your decision into action is under **Products | Settings** in your WordPress Dashboard:

Switch to the **Checkout** tab at the top of the page. On the **Checkout** page you will find an option to toggle between requiring users to register or not:

Setting it to **Yes** will enforce mandatory registration, but take note that you must also ensure that registration is enabled within WordPress (back in the general WordPress settings). Otherwise, you will effectively cut off customers from purchasing any products on your site. Ouch!

If you enforce customer registration, it's a great idea to create a test customer account to see how seamless or difficult the registration process is from the customer's perspective.

Creating a test customer account

Let's look at a few things from the customer's viewpoint. How much of a hassle is the registration process? Where is the order history located? Are there any complicated steps or issues?

Go ahead and log out from WordPress, or just open a different web browser. Browse to your site and imagine that you are looking at it through a customer's eyes. Add an item to your shopping cart and proceed through the checkout process. If mandatory registration is enabled, you should see a notice on the checkout page informing the new user that registration is necessary. Conveniently, they can create an account during the checkout process:

Not yet a member?

In order to buy from us, you'll need an account. Joining is free and easy. All you need is a username, password and valid email address.

Username:

Password:

E-mail:

This works very well for new customers, but what about returning ones? They still need to be able to log in before making purchases. On your site, how easy or difficult is it to find the *Log in* link? Your theme may have a prominent registration link in the header or footer, but if not, you can assist by making sure that the *Meta* widget is added to the sidebar, or by creating your own text widget with registration information within it.

Once registered customers return to your store and log in, they will eventually find themselves confronting the WordPress Dashboard. This presents a massive challenge for you as the store owner. Most of your customers are not likely to have any familiarity with WordPress, so suddenly finding themselves in the midst of the WordPress Dashboard may be startling for them. What, then, can we do to alleviate this problem?

Dealing with the WordPress Dashboard

In general, the fewer times customers need to see the WordPress Dashboard, the better. From a customer's perspective, it contains little useful and intuitive elements with regard to the online store. An ideal situation, for both you as the shop owner, and for your customers, is if they can avoid the Dashboard completely, even when they log in to their accounts. If only there were a way to automatically detect when a customer logs in and to redirect them somewhere other than to the Dashboard.

This is WordPress, after all, which means that there is likely to be an easy way to handle this situation. Fortunately, there is! Several third-party plugins exist that can help redirect logins, and we will describe two of them and how they can help here:

- Peter's Login Redirect
- Theme My Login

Redirect customer logins with 'Peter's Login Redirect'

One handy plugin for solving this problem is *Peter's Login Redirect* (`http://www.theblog.ca/wplogin-redirect`). It works by detecting a specific username, role, or permission level in WordPress, and then redirecting that user to a predetermined location. For our shop, all registered customers will have a WordPress role of *Subscriber*, so all we need to do is use this plugin to redirect all users with *Subscriber* roles to a URL of our choice.

Once you install and activate the plugin, you will see a link for **Login redirects** under **Settings** in your WordPress Dashboard:

Clicking on that link will allow you to create custom rules for how the plugin should redirect users upon successful login. Find the section on this page that handles **Specific roles**. Choose the **subscriber** role in the box next to the **Add** field:

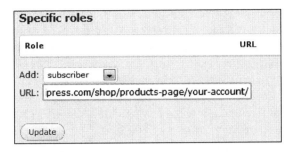

For the **URL**, we need to provide the full path to the customer account page, titled **Your Account**. The full path will vary depending on your permalink structure within WordPress, but is easy to discover. If in doubt, browse to your list of **Pages** in the Dashboard. The **Your Account** page is automatically added when you activate the WP e-Commerce plugin, and serves as a subpage of the **Products Page**. You can find the appropriate link by clicking on **View** underneath the **Your Account** subpage:

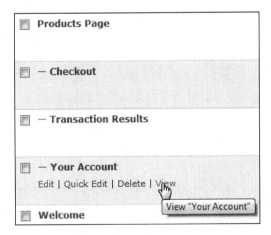

This is the URL that you must provide to *Peter's Login Redirect*. Click on the **Update** button to finish creating the redirect rule.

Try it now: log in to WordPress with your test customer account. If you created the rule correctly, you will find yourself automatically redirected to a personal account page, completely bypassing the Dashboard.

Dominate logins with 'Theme My Login'

If you really want full control over not only how customer login acts, but also how it looks, you owe it to yourself to consider the *Theme My Login* plugin (`http://bit.ly/theme-my-login`). Sure, it can handle login redirects, but it also does much more. One main feature is that it automatically detects the theme for your site and skins the *registration, login,* and *forgot password* pages within WordPress so that they look similar to the rest of your site. This can do wonders for customer confidence pertaining to how they interact with your store, as customers completely unfamiliar with WordPress may become alarmed or disconcerted when they try to register on your site and find themselves staring at a WordPress logo on a page that looks completely unrelated to your store. The *Theme My Login* plugin handles this for you without any manual intervention on your part.

Once you install and activate the plugin, you will find a link called **Theme My Login** underneath the **Settings** menu in the Dashboard:

Here are some suggestions for using *Theme My Login* in order to create a more seamless experience for customers:

- **Redirection**: Switch to the **Redirection** tab at the top of the *Theme My Login* settings page:

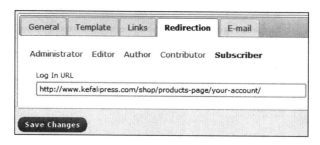

Just like with *Peter's Login Redirect* plugin, we need to specify the **Subscriber** role and add a **URL** where users with that role will be redirected upon a successful login. Be sure to click on **Save Changes** when you are finished.

- **Login widget**: The *Theme My Login* plugin comes with its own widget that you can add to your WordPress sidebar. This is great because it adds a customizable login screen to your store that also allows account registrations and password resets. The following screenshot shows what the expanded widget looks like in the Dashboard:

One neat option here is that you can set the **Default Action** to either **Login**, **Register**, or **Lost Password**. For our store, we will leave it set to **Login**, yet ensure that we have the checkboxes selected for **Allow Registration** and **Allow Password Recovery**. This will give our customers every option available directly in one place on any page of our online store.

The following screenshot shows the login widget in action:

- **Set links for post-login**: What happens after a customer logs in and shops for a while? What if she wants to return to her personal account page? Is it easy to find? One nice feature of the *Theme My Login* plugin is that you can configure it to automatically display a welcome message and show one or more links after a successful login. Best of all, you can configure what is displayed based on the user's role.

  Back on the *Theme My Login* settings page, switch to the **Links** tab at the top, and then choose the **Subscriber** role beneath it, as shown in the following screenshot:

We're going to create a link with the title **Your Account** and a URL to the customer account page. Now, when customers log in using the sidebar widget, they will see a welcome message and a link that they can use at any time to view their account details.

The following screenshot shows how it looks on our shop:

Both the *Theme My Login* and *Peter's Login Redirect* plugins offer a tremendous benefit: they help your customers avoid seeing the WordPress Dashboard. We strongly suggest using one of them in conjunction with WP e-Commerce.

Purchase history

As mentioned previously, one benefit of customer registration is that they have access to their full purchase history directly on your site. Once they log in, customers can view the **Your Account** page to gain access to their **Purchase History**, user Details, and digital download links:

As the **Your Account** page is a subpage of the **Products** Page, it might be easily viewable on your site, as shown in the following screenshot. Certain WordPress themes have easier access to subpages than others.

If you don't want to use one of the aforementioned login redirect plugins, another suggestion is to simply add a direct link to **Your Account** in a text widget on your site sidebar. When customers log in there instead of at the standard WordPress login prompt, they can also avoid the Dashboard entirely. The following screenshot shows the **Your Account** login page:

Summary

At this point you should have a pretty solid understanding of how WordPress handles multiple user accounts.

The following topics were covered in this chapter:

- Enabling user registration—turning on registration globally in WordPress
- Understand WordPress roles—the hierarchy of user permissions and capabilities
- Staff accounts—the two methods of registering staff members and setting their roles
- Customer accounts—considerations for whether or not to enforce customer registration
- Creating a test customer account—a look at the online store from a customer's viewpoint, including handling login redirects to avoid the Dashboard

You've also likely deduced that there are really three configuration possibilities with regard to additional users. They are:

- No registration—leave the WordPress global registration and the Checkout registration **OFF**
- Optional registration—leave the WordPress global registration **ON** and the Checkout registration **OFF**
- Mandatory registration—leave both the WordPress global registration and the Checkout registration **ON**

Any of the three possibilities could work well depending on how you wish to run your store. Now that your user settings are all configured, it's time to move to the exciting part: getting paid!

6
Checkout and Payment Setup

No e-commerce site is complete without a reliable way to accept payments from customers. Managing payments with the WP e-Commerce plugin is not a difficult process, but it is a process that must be tested thoroughly before opening your site to the public. After all, an online store with a broken payment system is totally worthless.

The nature of an online store inherently requires a fast and convenient method of accepting payments. For most users, this means the ability to accept credit or debit cards. Electronic checks are another option, though not all payment gateways support them.

There are other manual options available, such as allowing customers to send paper checks, but these are generally not recommended. Having customers mail checks is antiquated and can be risky. Therefore, if you have any other options available, we strongly recommend that you take advantage of them.

In this chapter, we will walk through the checkout process and decide how transparent we want the payment process to be for our customers. We will also explore the various payment gateways offered by the WP e-Commerce plugin, concluding with detailed instructions on setting up PayPal and Google Checkout.

This chapter covers:

- Planning the checkout process
- Available payment gateways
- Setting up PayPal Standard
- Setting up Google Checkout

Planning the checkout process

Before you can accept online payments directly from customers, there are a few things you should know. First of all, accepting credit card payments is not free. You will pay for the service one way or another. Either you can opt to pay a bank or company a setup fee plus a monthly or yearly fee for the necessary tools to accept credit cards online, or you will allow a payment processing service to take a small chunk of each transaction you receive for their service. The choice is yours, though many sole proprietors and small businesses find the latter option less painful mentally. Look at the fees that each service requires. If you have a high monthly sales volume, you may find the first option ultimately cheaper.

In either case, you will need to set up a payment gateway and/or a merchant account. What is the difference between the two? That's a good question, and many new shop owners are often confused by the difference, so let's cover it now.

Payment gateway versus merchant account

A payment gateway is simply a computer-driven service that authorizes a customer's credit or debit card, thus allowing for a collection of funds from that account. It also checks whether or not the card is legitimate.

A merchant account, on the other hand, is an account that you set up with a bank or other third-party company. The purpose of this account is to actually process credit or debit cards and transfer the funds to the bank account that you have arranged to receive those funds. Do you see the difference?

Picture yourself running errands. You need to pick up a few items for dinner tonight, so you visit the nearest grocery store. After you find your items and add them to your shopping basket, you head to the checkout lane. During checkout, you hand your credit card to the grocery clerk, who swipes it on a point-of-sale terminal. The terminal verifies that your card is valid and contains sufficient funds, and then communicates with a merchant account which actually withdraws the funds.

An online store works exactly the same way, with the exception that the payment gateway is a digital version of the point-of-sale terminal. The following image represents this idea:

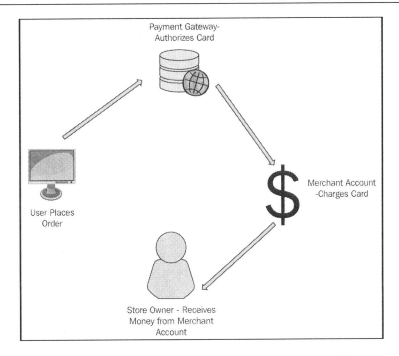

Certain payment gateways, notably Chronopay and Authorize.net, require that you also obtain a merchant account from a bank or other company. Other service providers, such as PayPal and Google Checkout, serve as both payment gateway and merchant account, thus eliminating the need for independent services. One system is not better or worse than the other. There are advantages either way.

Integration and checkout seamlessness

One fundamental decision that any shop owner must consider relates to the seamlessness of the checkout process. In other words, how integrated should the payment aspect be within the online store? When customers purchase items, should the entire transaction take place within the main site itself, so that customers are never even aware that a payment gateway is involved? Or should the transaction be visibly transferred to an external payment processor, such as PayPal?

Seamless integration is the main advantage of handling the transaction on the main site. Though it requires a more complicated setup process and higher upfront expenses, the result is a professional-looking checkout process where the customer adds items to the cart, enters payment details, and receives a payment confirmation notice, all without leaving the store website. Services such as Chronopay and Authorize.net offer this tight level of integration but with higher start up costs and monthly fees.

The less-seamless option is to pass the shopping cart information to an external service such as PayPal or Google Checkout. When customers go through the checkout process, they are visibly transferred to a third-party payment processor where they enter their payment information. Once the processor verifies their payment, they are redirected back to the seller's website. In this system, there are little-to-no upfront costs, but the integration is not as tight, either. On the other hand, the less-seamless option also has an advantage in that some customers may instinctively trust the entire process more because they recognize the payment processor (such as PayPal) and have faith that their payment details are secure.

Available payment gateways

The free version of the WP e-Commerce plugin offers access to several different payment gateways. They each have their own benefits and potential downsides, as well as pricing schemes. Purchasing the Gold Cart grants access to several additional gateways, most notably: Authorize.net.

The first step in choosing which gateway is right for you is to do your homework. Spend some time reading about the services offered by each gateway, as well as any limitations. Also, what fees does each gateway charge? Are the fees based on transaction, or are there additional setup and monthly fees involved?

In general, it's best to pick one gateway and stick with it. While it may sound tempting to offer several payment gateways to your customers, it also adds to potential customer confusion during the checkout process. Multiple gateways also complicate the set up and payment testing process, adding to the time required to launch your store and potentially creating conflicts between gateways. For instance, in earlier versions of the WP e-Commerce plugin, PayPal and Google Checkout did not coexist well, though a later plugin update fixed that problem.

To view the gateways available to you, navigate to your WordPress Dashboard, expand the **Products** section, and click on **Settings**, as shown in the following screenshot:

At the top of the page, click on the tab for **Payment Options**:

| General | Presentation | Admin | Shipping | Payment Options | Checkout |

You will see a listing of the available **Gateway Options**. Simply select the checkbox next to the gateway you wish to configure (as shown in the following screenshot) and click on the **Update** button. You should then see a number of options to configure for that gateway.

All of the payment gateways below are available in the free version of the plugin, with the exception of Authorize.net. The currently available gateways are:

- Chronopay
- Google Checkout
- Manual Payment / Test Gateway
- PayPal Payments Standard
- PayPal Express Checkout
- PayPal Payments Pro
- Authorize.net (Gold Cart only)

Chronopay

URL—`http://www.chronopay.com`

Based in Amsterdam, Chronopay is a reputable payment gateway for store owners based in the European Union. Like Authorize.net, Chronopay requires integration with a merchant account from an outside company.

Chronopay offers seamless integration with the shop owner's website, meaning that the entire transaction will occur without being transferred to an external site. This level of integration looks professional, but also requires the purchase of a Secure Sockets Layer (SSL) certificate from your web host.

Chronopay does not charge a setup fee or a recurring monthly fee, but they do charge a transaction-based fee starting at 2.00 percent + €0.30 per transaction. The addition of a merchant account will almost certainly cost a monthly fee, depending on the issuing bank.

Unfortunately for North American shop owners, Chronopay currently only issues accounts to sellers based mostly in European countries. For a full listing of countries, visit: `http://bit.ly/chronopay-acceptance`.

Google Checkout

URL—`http://checkout.google.com`

Launched in 2006, Google Checkout is a payment-processing service by Google designed to simplify how online payments work. Google Checkout is currently only available for sellers in the United States and the United Kingdom.

Google Checkout has interfaces for both buyers and sellers. For a buyer to use Google Checkout, he first stores his credit or debit card information, as well as a shipping address, inside a Google Account. In order to purchase items at online stores where Google Checkout is offered, the customer simply signs into his Google Account and makes the purchase, thus turning the transaction into practically a one-click affair.

For sellers, Google Checkout offers a convenient way to accept credit or debit cards with a Google Account. If a customer does not already have a Google Account, he may quickly create one without abandoning the current shopping cart. All transactions are handled securely on Google's servers, not on the seller's merchant site. However, the level of integration that Google Checkout provides requires that you have an SSL certificate available for your website.

Sellers must link an existing bank account to Google Checkout. When a customer purchases items from the seller, Google Checkout authorizes and charges the customer's credit or debit card, deducting a per-transaction fee from the total amount. Within a few days, Google then transfers the money directly to the seller's bank account, minus the small transaction fee.

Speaking of fees, the rates Google charges for payment processing is based on a tiered scale, determined by the monthly sales volume. Here is the tier of fees for US-based merchants:

Monthly Sales Through Google Checkout	Fees Per Transaction
Less than $3,000	2.9% + $0.30
$3,000 - $9,999.99	2.5% + $0.30
$10,000 - $99,999.99	2.2% + $0.30
$100,000 or more	1.9% + $0.30

As you can see, the more money you transact per month, the cheaper the rate becomes. There are no setup or monthly fees for using Google Checkout, you only have the per-transaction fee. The only exception is that Google charges an additional 1 percent fee if the buyer's home country differs from that of the seller.

To be clear, Google Checkout is available for buyers in most countries. However, only merchants based in the US or the UK can currently create seller accounts. Hopefully, this availability will expand in the future.

Manual Payment / Test Gateway

The Manual Payment / Test Gateway is really not a gateway at all. Instead, it's just a place-holder where a shop owner can leave instructions on how a customer can make a manual payment.

For instance, a shop owner could leave instructions on where to mail a paper check. He could also leave bank account information so a customer could make a direct deposit from another bank.

 Leaving direct deposit bank details on your site is a bad idea. Unfortunately, this behavior is still practiced in certain regions of the world.

More commonly, this option is solely used for testing purposes. If you leave this option as the only payment method, you can test the behavior and functionality of your shopping cart by completing as many purchases as you like. Just be sure to switch to a different gateway before your site goes live.

PayPal Payments Standard

URL—http://www.paypal.com

Acquired by eBay in 2002, PayPal is perhaps the largest and most recognized payment processor in the world. Due to a turbid past, it is also the most criticized. That said, PayPal has been around since the dawn of the 21st century and is available in over 190 countries, making it a sound choice for a default payment gateway.

For buyers, PayPal offers a convenient way to pay for items by using either a credit or debit card, an electronic check, or from their existing PayPal balance. Customers do not need a PayPal account in order to purchase from online stores where PayPal is offered (depending on the country in which the seller is located).

For sellers, PayPal offers a myriad of options. There are three account types available: Personal, Premier, and Business. The Personal account is worthless from a shop-owner's perspective as it does not allow acceptance of credit cards. Both the Premier and Business account types allow for acceptance of credit cards. The main difference between them is that a Business account allows a merchant to operate under a company name instead of a person's name (as with the Premier account).

As far as integration with the WP e-Commerce plugin goes, there are three choices available: PayPal Payments Standard, PayPal Express Checkout, and PayPal Payments Pro.

All transactions using PayPal Payments Standard are handled on PayPal's servers, not on the seller's merchant site, thus eliminating the need for an SSL certificate. When customers want to purchase items, the WP e-Commerce plugin transfers the shopping cart information to PayPal, where the customer pays for the items. After the transaction is complete, PayPal returns the customer to the seller's online store.

Concerning fees, PayPal Payments Standard has no setup or monthly fees. Instead, it operates on a tiered, per-transaction fee identical to that of Google Checkout:

Purchase payments received (monthly)	Fee per transaction
$0.00 USD - $3,000.00 USD	2.9% + $0.30 USD
$3,000.01 USD - $10,000.00 USD	2.5% + $0.30 USD
$10,000.01 USD - $100,000.00 USD	2.2% + $0.30 USD
> $100,000.00 USD	1.9% + $0.30 USD†

PayPal Express Checkout

The main difference between Express Checkout and Website Payments Standard is that Express Checkout requires that customers already have a PayPal account. When a customer makes a purchase on your site, he is automatically directed to PayPal, where he confirms his payment method and shipping address, then commits to the purchase. Express Checkout also requires that the seller have a Business account with PayPal.

There are no additional fees for Express Checkout, and the same per-transaction rates apply as those for Website Payments Standard.

PayPal Payments Pro

If you want PayPal to handle all of your transactions, but also want seamless integration with your website, then PayPal Payments Pro is right for you. From the customer's perspective, the entire transaction is handled directly on your site and there is no visible third party involved. All credit or debit card payments are processed behind the scenes by PayPal.

A Payments Pro account also comes with PayPal's Virtual Terminal, allowing you to accept credit or debit card payments over the phone, by fax, or in person. These features are impressive, but you will need to pay a $30 monthly fee for a Payments Pro account, in addition to the standard PayPal fee per transaction.

Authorize.net

URL—`http://authorize.net`

Established in 1996, Authorize.net is a payment gateway that also requires a merchant account with an outside company. While Authorize.net is undoubtedly more expensive upfront than other gateways such as PayPal, it also allows for complete and seamless integration with your online store.

Using what they call an **Advanced Integration Method (AIM)**, Authorize.net allows a merchant's website to hook into its API and process transactions without leaving the original site. From a customer's perspective, everything is seamless. The customer proceeds to the checkout page and enters payment or shipping information all on the merchant's website without being visibly shuffled to a third-party payment processor.

Such convenience looks professional, but it will cost you. Purchased directly from the source, Authorize.net requires a $99 setup fee, plus a $20 monthly fee to remain active. Each transaction also has a $0.10 fee. The Authorize.net gateway is also available from numerous resellers, though fees may vary.

Because the entire transaction is handled on your online store, your website will also need an SSL certificate, which is available from your web host. A dedicated SSL certificate currently costs between $30 to $50 a year.

Setting up PayPal Standard

For our sheet music shop, we are going to stick with a standard PayPal account. It's simple, it works, and it doesn't require any upfront costs. Since the transaction is handled securely on PayPal's server, we don't need to worry about purchasing and setting up an SSL certificate. When it comes down to it, PayPal offers the fastest, most convenient, and least-troublesome integration with the WP e-Commerce plugin. To continue, you will need either a Premier or a Business account with PayPal. If you don't already have one, go ahead and sign up for one now by going to www.paypal.com and clicking on the **Sign up** link. There are no setup or monthly costs involved.

Setting up PayPal with the e-Commerce plugin is easy. Setting up and *testing to make sure it works* takes a little more time, but is absolutely required in order to make sure your store functions properly. Just think of how many sales you could lose if you release your store to the public with a broken payment system.

To show how easy it is to set up integration with PayPal, the following is all that is required.

Under the **Payment Options** tab, choose **PayPal Payments Standard** as your sole gateway. When the configuration options load, change the PayPal **Username** to the e-mail address associated with your PayPal account:

That's it. Click on the **Update** button and you're done. The rest of the necessary configuration should be pre-filled for you, such as the **PayPal URL**. These are the settings to which we will return later, but for now, we need to do some testing. Is there more to it than that? Yes, but this is all that is necessary on the WordPress side of things. There is more that you must do within PayPal itself, but we'll cover that in the discussion of the sandbox.

Playing in the sandbox

In order to fully test a transaction without spending any real money, you should sign up for a PayPal Developer account at: `https://developer.paypal.com`.

A free Developer account provides us with a "sandbox" environment, which will allow us to make as many test transactions as we want. At no point will any real money change hands, but we can see exactly how the entire transaction process works. What is especially important about this is that it lets us see how our online store handles any post-transaction elements, such as confirmation notices and delivery of digital downloads.

Within the PayPal Developer account, you can create two (or more) test accounts: one to represent a merchant and one to represent a test buyer. To create these accounts, first navigate to the **Test Accounts** section within the **Sandbox** menu:

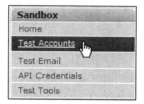

In the page that loads, look for the **Create Account** section. You have two choices: to create a **Preconfigured** account (easiest) or use the **Create Manually** option. No matter which option you select, keep in mind that you will need test accounts for both a buyer and a seller. Set up the test accounts in the sandbox and remember what they are, as you will need them again shortly:

Your test buyer shows up as having a **Personal** account, and should have a **per** somewhere in the e-mail address. The test seller shows up as having a **Business** account, with a **biz** somewhere within the email address.

WP e-Commerce Payment settings

Back on the WordPress Dashboard for your online store, re-visit the **Payment Options** tab for your PayPal settings and make these changes:

1. Set the PayPal **Username** to the e-mail address of the test Business account.

2. Set the PayPal **Url** to: `https://www.sandbox.paypal.com/cgi-bin/webscr`, as shown in the following screenshot:

 Remember that these settings are for testing purposes only and should be changed back to your regular PayPal information before officially launching your site.

Setting up IPN

Notice that so far we have left **PayPal IPN** set to **Yes**. What is **IPN**? It stands for **Instant Payment Notification**, and it is PayPal's interface for handling real-time purchase confirmation and server-to-server communication. Simply put, it allows PayPal to notify your online store that a customer has successfully purchased and paid for an item. It makes your life easier when it comes to recording sales back on your own site instead of looking at PayPal all of the time.

There are a few things we need to do to ensure that IPN is fully working with our site, so let's go back to our Developer Sandbox. All of the following configuration settings are within PayPal.

 You are modifying these settings in the Sandbox. Before launching your store, be sure to re-create the same changes to your *real* PayPal account.

On the **Test Accounts** page within your Developer account, click on the radio button next to your test Business account and then click on **Enter Sandbox Test Site**.

It will launch a new browser window that looks just like the regular PayPal website, but with the word "Sandbox" at the top. Log in with your test Business account e-mail and password. Once logged in, your test account looks and acts like a regular PayPal account, with the exception that all of the money and payment details are fake.

Click on the **Profile** link near the top to view your test account's profile. Below, you should see a list of **Selling Preferences**, as shown in the following screenshot:

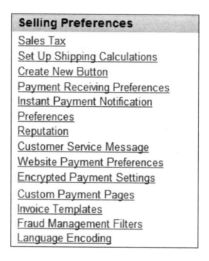

Click on the link for **Instant Payment Notification**. You will see an option to enable IPN, and once you do so, you will be able tell PayPal to **Receive IPN messages**, plus add a **Notification URL:**

Enable **IPN messages**, and for the **Notification URL**, specify the full URL to your site with **?ipn_request=true** added to the end.

Be sure to click on **Save** when finished. Congratulations, IPN is now enabled, and PayPal can communicate more effectively with your online store.

Set up Auto Return

There's one last thing to do before we try a test transaction. We should set up Auto Return within PayPal. The main purpose of Auto Return is to improve integration by automatically re-routing a customer back to your online store after he completes his payment with PayPal. This is essential because it shows the customer the Transaction Results, plus any links for digital downloads.

For more information on Auto Return visit `http://bit.ly/auto-return`.

You can find the configuration for Auto Return in the PayPal profile for your test Business account. Click on the link for **Website Payment Preferences**.

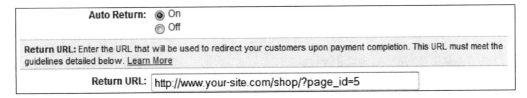

As seen above, you have the option to enable **Auto Return**, plus provide a **Return URL**. The **Return URL** is the link to which PayPal should deliver the customer once the payment has been processed. This should be the full URL for your Transaction Results page.

If in doubt as to the path of your Transaction Results page, navigate to **Pages** in your WordPress Dashboard and click on the **View** link under **Transaction Results**. This will show you the full URL:

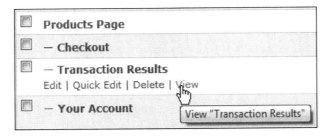

One more thing to note, while still on the *Website Payment Preferences* page, scroll down to the **Payment Data Transfer** section and switch it to **On**, as shown in the following screenshot:

Payment Data Transfer (optional)

Payment Data Transfer allows you to receive notification of successful payments as they are made. The use of Payment Data Transfer depends on your system configuration and your Return URL. Please note that in order to use Payment Data Transfer, you **must** turn on Auto Return.

    Payment Data Transfer: ⦿ On
                                      ○ Off

In conjunction with IPN, **Payment Data Transfer (PDT)** helps ensure that all of the details of the transaction are displayed to the customer upon return to the **Transaction Results**.

The test transaction

You have now completed the necessary steps to integrate PayPal with the WP e-Commerce plugin. However, the setup is not complete until you have tested the payment system to make sure it works!

When initiating the test transaction be sure to first log into your PayPal Developer account, then open a new browser tab or window to visit your online store. If you attempt the test transaction without first logging into your Developer account, the transaction will likely fail due to PayPal's re-routing to the main Developer login.

Go ahead and try to buy an item from yourself. When you come to the **Billing and Shipping Information** section, enter the **test Personal** email address that you set up in the PayPal Developer Sandbox (the one that has a **per** in it). That's the important part. Throw in some random information for the other entries, such as address and phone number.

When you confirm the order, you will be taken to the Sandbox. Log in with the test Personal e-mail address and password that you created, and proceed with the transaction:

Don't worry, you are not actually spending real money. When finished, if all goes as planned, you should automatically be returned to your **Transaction Results** page. If your mock purchase included a digital download, you should see a download link, as shown by the **Click to download** link displayed in the following screenshot:

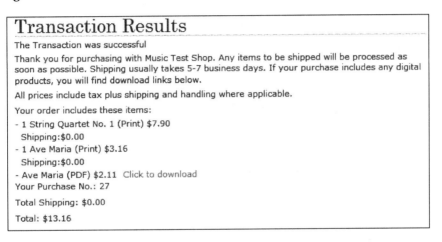

This completes our setup of PayPal Payments Standard. When you have finished testing, the most critical issue to remember before your site goes live is to switch PayPal's configuration from the "sandbox" back into production mode.

Setting up Google Checkout

If you are dissatisfied with PayPal, or want to offer an alternative payment gateway in conjunction with PayPal, then we recommend Google Checkout. As with PayPal, there are no monthly fees; you only have a pay a small, per-transaction fee. Keep in mind that as of this writing, Google Checkout is only available for sellers in the United States and the United Kingdom, though customers can purchase items from almost any country. Google Checkout will hopefully be available in more countries in the future.

As with PayPal, configuring Google Checkout to work with WP e-Commerce is quick and simple, while configuring *and testing* takes a little more time and effort. Still, if you want to use Google Checkout, it is imperative that you take the time to test every component of the transaction process yourself. After all, you want to ensure that your customers can pay you, right?

To illustrate how simple the initial configuration for Google Checkout is, just follow these easy steps. First, go back in your WP e-Commerce settings, switch to the **Payment Options** tab and select Google Checkout as your sole or additional gateway. Next, when the configuration options load, add your **Merchant ID** and **Merchant Key** in the appropriate fields:

If you are unsure where to find those values, you can find them by logging into your Google Checkout account and clicking on **Settings**, then **Integration**.

Next, choose your desired currency from the **Select your currency** drop-down box. At present, only USD and GBP are available. Finally, be sure to select a list of countries to which you are willing to ship by clicking on the **Set Shipping countries** link.

For now, that's basically all you need to do. Be sure to click on the **Update** button to save your settings.

Playing in Google's sandbox

Just like in our description of setting up PayPal, we need a way to test our transactions without having to spend any real money. Fortunately, Google offers a free "sandbox" environment in order to do just that. To use the sandbox, you will need to create two additional accounts, one for the test buyer and one for the test seller:

1. Test buyer account—`https://sandbox.google.com/checkout`

2. Test seller account— `https://sandbox.google.com/checkout/sell`

You must sign up for each account separately. Creating a test buyer account will not automatically create a test seller account, and vice-versa. Keep in mind that you will still need to provide a credit card number for the buyer account, though it need not be legitimate. Refer to the following paragraphs for some sample numbers.

Also, there's one potential hurdle when creating your seller account: Google requires that you confirm your identity by entering a verification code that you will receive by SMS (text message). You can still sign up even if you don't have a mobile phone, but you will need to ask a friend if you can use his number to verify the SMS code.

With our new sandbox accounts in hand, we can safely test our transactions all day long without exchanging any real money. It also gives us a first-hand view of how the purchasing process will appear to our customers, including any e-mail confirmations and delivering of any digital downloads.

When creating your test accounts, keep in mind that the process is exactly the same as creating a regular Google Checkout account, and you are welcome to use the same login information as an existing Google account. If you wish to create your login information from scratch, take note that the only valid information Google requires is an e-mail address and (naturally) a password. The rest of the information, such as address and phone number, can be completely fabricated.

Speaking of fabrication, you will need to provide a credit or debit card number for your test buyer account. In the sandbox, no transactions will actually be processed, but you still must provide a number. Just as with the address and phone number, the credit card number that you provide does not need to be valid. Here are a few sample credit card numbers that are available for testing purposes:

- VISA – 4111 1111 1111 1111
- MasterCard – 5500 0000 0000 0004
- American Express – 3400 0000 0000 009

No, these are not real credit card numbers. They are numbers offered by their respective vendors for testing transactions. Your "test buyer" Google Checkout account should happily accept one of these sample numbers. Here is a screenshot of the financial details for my test buyer account in Google Checkout, complete with a fabricated name, address, and phone number:

WP e-Commerce Payment settings

With our test buyer and seller accounts created in Google Checkout, we can continue our configuration. Browse back to your WordPress Dashboard and re-visit the **Payment Options** tab for your Google Checkout settings. Here you will need to update your **Merchant ID** and **Merchant Key** information with the values provided in your test seller account. Also, be sure to switch the **Server Type** to **Sandbox (For testing)**:

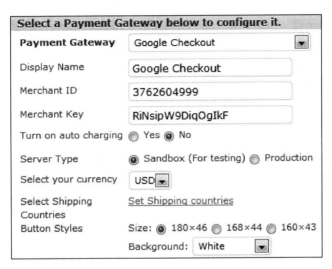

You can find the appropriate values by logging into your Google Checkout "test seller" account and clicking on the **Settings** tab and then clicking on **Integration**:

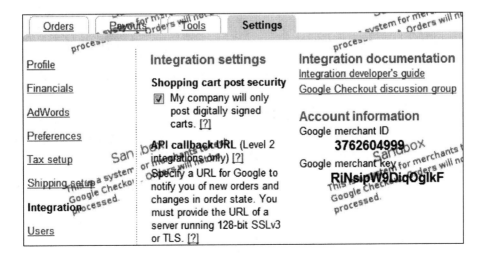

Remember that these settings are for testing purposes only and should be changed back to your regular Google Checkout information before officially launching your site.

We have one other setting to consider back on the **Payment Gateway** page. That is whether or not the **Turn on auto charging** option should be enabled or disabled. If it is enabled, whenever a customer completes a payment, Google Checkout will go ahead and charge their credit or debit card for the full amount. If left disabled, Google Checkout will require you to manually verify the transaction before charging the card. It's an added step, but some people prefer it that way. The choice is yours.

Google integration settings

Before we proceed with a test transaction, we have one remaining issue to address. This is not necessarily relevant to the Google Checkout sandbox, but will be for the production environment. The issue is that in order to fully integrate with your online store, Google Checkout requires you to provide them with an API callback URL. This callback URL is what notifies your online store of purchases and allows the WP e-Commerce plugin to keep track of transaction history. Fortunately, WP e-Commerce automatically provides you with the link. All you need to do is copy and paste that link into your Google Checkout seller account:

There are two important issues to note here. First, the integration that the callback URL offers requires that you have a **Secure Sockets Layer (SSL)** certificate available on your server. These can cost anywhere from $30 to $50 or more per year, depending on where you purchase them. We have teamed with GoDaddy to offer one-year SSL certificates for $12.99 (http://bit.ly/ssl-godaddy).

Once your certificate is installed and working, we need to browse to our Google Checkout seller (non-test) account and select **Settings**, then **Integration**. In the **API callback URL** section, paste the link that WP e-Commerce provided, with one slight modification. Instead of http://, change the beginning to read **https://**. This change can be seen in the following screenshot:

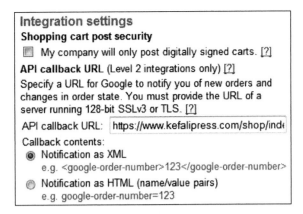

 Remember that this is only necessary when Google Checkout is in production mode. It is not necessary for sandbox testing.

The test transaction

You have now completed the necessary steps to integrate Google Checkout with the WP e-Commerce plugin. All that remains is to attempt a test transaction in order to ensure that everything is working properly. Go ahead and try to buy something from yourself. When you proceed to checkout, you will see that you are able to **Select a payment gateway**. These gateways can be seen in the following screenshot:

After we click on the **Make Purchase** button, the **Google Checkout** link is now available:

When we proceed with the purchase, we are prompted to log into our Google account. Here is where we enter the information for our test buyer, as seen in the following screenshot:

Finally, we are taken to the Google Checkout sandbox and presented with a summary of our soon-to-be-placed order. Here we can see the phony shipping information and the sample credit card details:

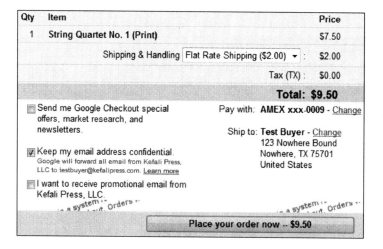

All that is left is to click on the **Place your order now** button. When complete, you should see a confirmation from Google that your order was successful:

Of course, this entire transaction has been handled in the sandbox, and no actual money has changed hands. When you switch back to production mode, it is a good idea to test this process again, including potentially creating an extremely inexpensive item that you purchase from yourself, or have a friend purchase from you. You can always cancel the order from within your Google Checkout seller control panel. Peace of mind that the process works is worth any potential hassle.

Summary

At this point, you should have a solid understanding of how the checkout process works, plus have a general awareness of the positives and negatives of the various payment processing services available.

You should also feel comfortable integrating at least one payment gateway into your online store. If in doubt, PayPal is a solid option due to its near-worldwide availability and its relative simplicity.

No matter which gateway you choose, be sure to test it thoroughly before releasing it to the public.

This chapter covered:

- Planning the checkout process
- Available payment gateways—an overview of available payment processors, including fees.
- Setting up PayPal Standard—detailed instructions on integrating PayPal Website Payments (Standard) with the WP e-Commerce plugin
- Setting up Google Checkout

Now that you have a functioning payment setup, let's continue our store-building process. Up next, we'll cover specifics on shipping, taxes, and processing orders.

7
Shipping, Taxes, and Processing Orders

By this point, the majority of your initial store assembly is complete. You have configured your initial settings, built your product catalog, and set up at least one payment gateway. Still, there is more work to do. In the previous chapter, we made it possible to accept payment online for the products that we sell, but we also need to get the product to the customer in the most efficient and inexpensive way possible, then navigate the maelstrom of tax laws to stay within the legal confines of our home state or country.

In this chapter, we will discuss the elements that concern us during and after a customer goes through the checkout process. These essential elements include tax configuration, shipping settings, and e-mail issues. We will also walk through a complete transaction from customer and store-owner perspectives, testing all variables. Despite our best efforts to construct a perfect system, we may find a flaw somewhere during the process.

This chapter covers:

- Locations and tax setup
- Shipping Options and Calculators
- Processing a test order
- E-mails sent to you and the customer
- Sales log

Effectively, what we want to ensure is that the entire checkout process works smoothly for all involved. We want to ensure that any applicable taxes and shipping charges are calculated correctly, and that both the customer and store owner receive accurate notifications about any orders. Be sure to test these processes thoroughly—the last thing you want to do is hurt your business by keeping customers uninformed or by under or overcharging for taxes and shipping.

Locations and tax setup

We touched on this topic briefly back in Chapter 3, but it's appropriate to discuss taxes and locations further. There's no doubt that tax law is complicated, but it's a necessity. It's far beyond the scope of this book to discuss tax law in all countries, so be sure to do your own research regarding taxes for your own state, country, and region.

For businesses located in the USA, here are a couple of links to get you started:

- Amazon Sales Tax Info – `http://bit.ly/amazon-sales-tax`
- State Tax Info – `http://www.business.gov/finance/taxes/state.html`

Within the USA, most businesses charge state sales tax based on the *shipping* information that the customer provides. While nine times out of ten a customer's billing and shipping information are the same, the times when the billing and shipping information differ can lead to some interesting scenarios.

For example, if your store is based in Kansas, a customer in Kansas who buys a product and ships it to Texas would *not* have to pay tax on that order, at least not to the state of Kansas. On the other hand, a customer in Georgia who buys your product and ships it to Kansas *would* have to pay tax on the order. Again, tax law is undoubtedly complicated, so be sure to look up any laws specific to your own state.

On to business—the first thing to do is to verify that your **Base Country/Region** is correct. You can find this under the **General** tab of the WP e-Commerce Plugin Settings, as seen in the following screenshot:

Next, verify that the tax percentages are correct for your state or region. This is just underneath the settings for **Base Country/Region**.

Finally, switch to the **Checkout** tab at the top to consider one more setting. Just under **Checkout Options**, there is an option to **Lock Tax to Billing Country**. This is shown in the following screenshot:

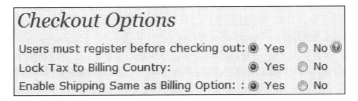

What this option does, once selected, is lock the billing country to the shipping country. For stores in the USA, it also has the effect of locking the billing *state* to the shipping *state*. This certainly simplifies matters, but it doesn't quite solve the tax scenarios outlined earlier in this section.

Shipping Options and Calculators

Configuring a store's shipping options is potentially one of the most complicated tasks that new store owners face, but it doesn't have to be. Much of it depends on the type of products that you are planning to sell. The absolute simplest scenario involves selling digital downloads only, in which case you don't need to worry about shipping at all.

When dealing with tangible goods, one's shipping needs grow increasingly complicated depending on the diversity of the products involved and anticipated location of the customers. For instance, selling books as well as clothing will create different shipping needs than selling only books *or* clothing. Also, planning to sell to customers worldwide will necessitate more complicated shipping needs than limiting one's customer base to only one or two countries.

Unlike creating and modifying a product catalog, configuring shipping settings is a task that only needs to be done once.

General Shipping Settings

To view and modify your shipping settings, switch to the **Shipping** tab at the top of the **Settings** page, as seen in the following screenshot:

Under the **General Settings**, you have the option to globally enable or disable shipping. If your shop is comprised of digital downloads only, then you can safely switch the **Use Shipping** option to **No** and rejoice! You no longer have to worry about any shipping configuration. The following screenshot shows the relevant panel:

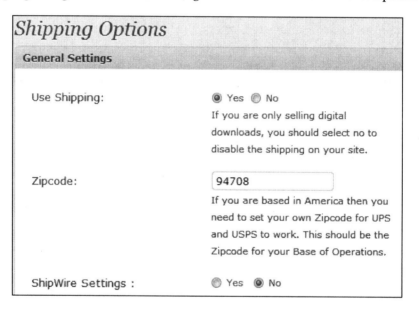

Those, who do sell tangible items should leave it set to **Yes,** as shown above. If your store is located in the USA, add the **Zipcode** for the area from where you will be shipping items. This is really only necessary if you plan to use one of the external shipping calculators (UPS or USPS), but it doesn't hurt to add it anyway.

If you subscribe to the third-party Shipwire order fulfillment service (www.shipwire.com), set the Shipwire option to **Yes** and enter your relevant login information. Shipwire is a service that collects and stores your products for you, shipping them to customers when necessary. While convenient, Shipwire comes with a cost, currently starting at $30 per month.

One neat aspect of the e-Commerce plugin is that you can opt to allow for free shipping, provided that the order price is above a certain threshold. At the bottom of the general shipping options is a toggle to **Enable Free Shipping Discount**, as seen in the following screenshot:

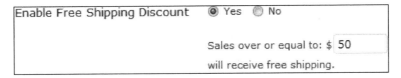

Enter a threshold amount of your choice, such as **$50**, like seen above. Any orders that customers place with a value equal to or higher than that price will automatically qualify for free shipping.

Shipping Modules

The WP e-Commerce plugin comes with five different shipping modules (three internal and two external) to help calculate shipping. Altogether, they give you a lot of variety with regards to controlling shipping charges. They include:

- Flat Rate
- Table Rate
- Weight Rate
- UPS (external)
- USPS (external)

So, what is the difference between these modules? The first thing you must do when deciding how to calculate shipping is sit back and consider the nature of the items you are selling. How heavy is each item? Are all of your products approximately the same weight? Will you likely be shipping to the same geographical area, or are your planned shipping distances more diverse? Once you have considered shipping weights and distance, you can decide upon a shipping strategy that suits your needs.

No matter which shipping module you ultimately choose, you can edit the settings for that particular module by hovering your mouse over it. An **Edit** link will appear to the right-hand side of the module, as shown in the following screenshot:

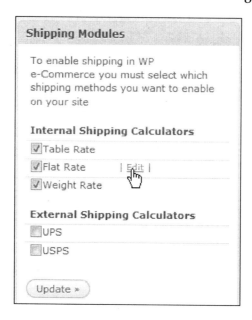

Keep in mind that you are by no means limited to one shipping module. You can offer several different modules if you like, but more does not necessarily equate better in this case. Offering many different ways to calculate shipping has the potential to confuse the customer, who will opt for the cheapest shipping method in most cases.

Flat Rate

Setting a flat rate for shipping is the simplest option, but will not work for all situations. A flat rate is exactly what it sounds like—customers pay one predetermined fee for shipping, based upon their location, regardless of the number of items purchased and the total price of the order. A customer in the United States might pay one set shipping charge, whereas a customer in Europe will pay a different set price. As the store owner, you have control over the shipping charges you set for each region.

The **Flat Rate** itself has a **Base** price, which you can set as high or low as you like, as well as an optional per-item charge. For your home country, you can set a **Base Local** price. Customers within your home country will automatically have that Base Local fee added to their entire order, whether they purchase a single item or a hundred. Most countries will only have a single entry for the **Base Local** price, but some countries may have multiple spaces. For instance, if your home country is set to the USA, you will have local options for the **Continental 48 States** as well as **All 50 States**, as seen in the following screenshot:

If you plan to ship internationally, you can set base prices for international customers. Keep in mind that the **Base International** prices are independent from the **Base Local** prices, not added on top of them. With the flat rates shown in the previous screenshot, customers in Hawaii would have $2 added to their entire order, while customers in Greece would have $4 added to the exact same order.

While setting a Flat Rate is a simple option overall, there are ways to get more advanced usage. You can also set a *per-item* fee on top of that flat rate. Imagine this scenario: Maria visits your shop to buy a few things. Your shop has a base shipping rate of $5, so Maria will be charged at least $5 for shipping no matter what, even if she buys fifty items from you. Let's also say that each of your items has a *per-item* shipping fee of $1. In this case, the formula for calculating shipping is now:

[base fee] + [per-item fee * number of items]

If Maria adds a single item to her cart, the total shipping fee will be **$6** ($5 + $1). If she adds four items to her cart, the new shipping fee will be **$9** ($5 + $4).

This is a straightforward example involving a universal fee per item, but you can set a wide variety of fees per item if you want.

You can set *per-item* shipping fees for each item back on the **Products** page. While editing the details for that particular product, scroll down to the **Shipping Details**, as seen below:

In this example, we set a $1 fee per item shipped within the home country, and a $1.75 fee per item shipped internationally. Keep in mind that this is on top of the base fee per order.

If you opt for Flat Rate shipping, feel free to use your imagination. Any combination of base rate plus item fees is possible. You may find that having a base rate of $0 and relying solely upon per-item fees works best for you. Or, you may find that only a handful of heavy items should have individual fees. The possibilities are practically limitless.

Table Rate

Using Table Rate for shipping provides a handy way to set various tiers for the total shipping cost. Essentially, it allows you to set price ranges that have a predetermined shipping cost, no matter what the type or number of items involved. Total cost of the products in the shopping cart determines the shipping amount.

When configuring your **Table Rate**, you create multiple layers to form a shipping cost hierarchy. The following is an example:

Each *layer* has a required value relating to the **Total Price** for the order and the resulting **Shipping Price**. In this example, we are going to reward our customers for making larger purchases by consistently reducing the shipping cost as the price of the total order increases. We do this in layers: the most expensive shipping ($6) is for orders under $20. As the order price increases, the shipping decreases, ultimately resulting in free shipping for orders above $50.

This is only one possible use of layers in your rate table. One simplified version of this solution is to have only two layers, granting free shipping over a specified price. There are many possibilities, and you can create as many layers as you like.

Weight Rate

Similar to Table Rate, specifying **Weight Rate** as your shipping module allows you to create layers to form a hierarchy of shipping costs. The difference is that instead of being based on total order cost, the hierarchy is based on the weight of the items, with the general idea that the heavier the order, the more it will cost to ship:

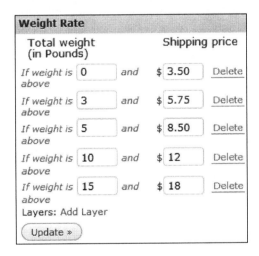

In this example, orders with total weights under three pounds will have a shipping charge of $3.50. As the weight increases, the price increases accordingly, with the heaviest orders (over fifteen pounds) weighing in at a hefty shipping price of $18.

In order for **Weight Rate** to work as a viable shipping option, you must specify a weight for each individual item. You can do this back on the **Products** page. Just like when adding a per-item fee for the **Flat Rate** module, view the details for a specific product and scroll down to the **Shipping Details,** as seen in the following screenshot:

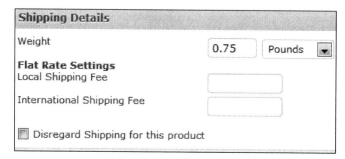

Here you can add a weight for each item. In this example, we have set a weight of **0.75 Pounds** for this item. If a customer adds multiples of this same item to his cart, the weight will increase accordingly and will be combined with the differing weights of other products in the customer's cart.

Of course, if you would rather not deal with pounds, you could always click on the drop-down menu to switch to another unit of mass, such as **Ounces**, **Grams**, or **Kilograms**, as shown in the following screenshot:

Unfortunately, this unit change will *not* be reflected back on the **Weight Rate** layer configuration page. As of this writing, the various layers must be constructed using only **Pounds** as the unit of mass.

Using an external Shipping Calculator

The WP e-Commerce plugin supports integration with UPS and USPS. As these are both third-party services, you should create an account with one or the other before you can offer them as valid shipping options.

Using one of these services relieves you of some of the burden of determining how much shipping to charge. UPS or USPS will calculate it exactly for you and present the cost to the customer during checkout.

UPS Calculator

The UPS Shipping Calculator differs from USPS in that it does not actually require you to create an account with them. Plugging into the UPS system is as easy as selecting the appropriate checkbox and editing the settings for this module, as seen in the following screenshot:

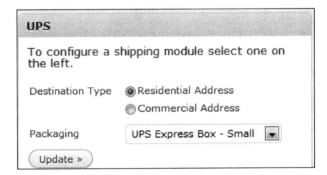

To have UPS calculate shipping for you, you have to give them a couple of default values. Specifically, you must inform them of whether your intended destinations will be **Residential** or **Commercial** addresses. You must also indicate the default size of your shipping materials, such as a letter or a medium-sized box.

UPS calculations are partly based on weight, so in order to accurately calculate shipping costs, your products must have an associated weight. If you are using variations for your products, be sure to add a weight to each individual variation. Otherwise, you will see a red exclamation point next to each product in the WordPress Dashboard.

Let's see this in action: assuming that our store is based in the USA, here is what would happen when a customer from elsewhere in the world visits your store. Instead of you having to worry about how much it will cost to ship a product abroad, UPS handles it for you. This is demonstrated in the following screenshot:

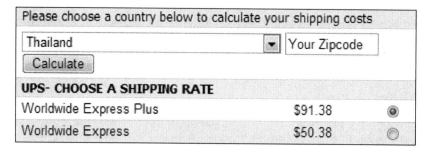

Even though the customer might recoil in horror at the cost of shipping, at least you, as the store owner, know that it is covered and that you will not lose a boatload of money on shipping costs. Assuming the customer selects UPS and makes the purchase, all that is left for you to do is to make contact with UPS and confirm the shipping details. If you plan to offer UPS, you should create an account with them in order to enjoy other benefits, such as automated pick-up service. Create your account at www.ups.com.

While convenient, one disadvantage is that UPS shipping can be expensive, sometimes painfully so. Be sure to do your research before committing—you may find that another service suits your needs better.

USPS Calculator

Integrating USPS shipping requires that you register for their Web Tools service. Start here: http://www.usps.com/webtools

Once you register, you will receive an automated e-mail with your account user ID and password that describes how to start using their service. It will include detailed information on how to communicate with their servers, but fortunately, the WP e-Commerce plugin already handles this integration.

> The critical part of integrating USPS is as follows:
>
> When you have completed your testing, email the USPS **Internet Customer Care Center** (**ICCC**). They will switch your profile to allow you access to the production server and will provide you with the production URLs.
>
> The ICCC is staffed from 7:00AM to 11:00PM Eastern Time.
>
> E-mail: icustomercare@usps.com
>
> Telephone: 1-800-344-7779

As you can see, completing your shop's integration with USPS takes a little time. After you first create your account, you will receive your account information by e-mail. You must then contact them again to request permission to access the production server instead of the testing server. If you contact USPS by e-mail, be sure to mention your account username, and also that you are using the WP e-Commerce plugin as your shopping cart script. Otherwise, they are likely to cause a further delay by asking you to verify one or the other. Once they grant permission, you can successfully start using USPS on your site.

The actual integration process is simple—all you have to do is add your unique user ID and password to the USPS settings, as follows:

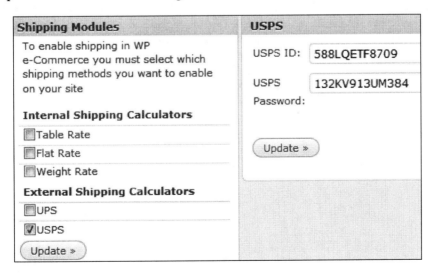

The WP e-Commerce plugin will handle the rest.

Processing a test order

Now that you have set up a payment gateway, added your tax settings, and configured one or more shipping modules, it's time to put the entire collective together and verify that everything works! You can do this by walking through the entire process from a customer's perspective and seeing what happens (or what should happen) from the store owner's point of view.

Before you begin the testing process, it's important to emphasize that you should use multiple web browsers when testing your site. Not all browsers render websites in the same manner, and since we are planning to cater to customers worldwide, we must verify that our site works with a variety of browsers.

Testing that your site works involves much more than adding a single product to your shopping cart—you need to verify that all cart actions work, such as adding dozens of products, emptying the cart, verifying tax and shipping settings, and ensuring that all the correct information is sent to the selected payment gateway.

This is a big task, one that you must take very seriously. Don't assume anything works correctly unless you have verified it yourself. There could be an undiscovered bug in the software, or your WordPress theme might do something wacky. You need to view each page and product yourself to ensure that it works. There's no substitute for a methodical testing progression.

Tempting though it may be to try to immediately fix a bug or an inappropriate setting with your store, it's better to simply make a note of it and continue the testing process. Multiple problems may have the same related cause, and you can be more efficient with your fixes if you have already seen the big picture.

Here is a checklist of actions that you should try at this point:

Store testing checklist

Check all WordPress pages:

- Any broken links?
- Do pages render properly in multiple browsers?
- If you have a Contact Form, does it work?

Check all Product links:

- Any broken links?
- Do Categories or Tags work properly?
- Do Variations work (if needed)?
- Do Breadcrumbs work (if enabled)?
- Do image thumbnails display on Products or Groups?
- Does Pagination work?
- Is your Permalink structure appropriate?

Check the Shopping Cart:

- Can you add items to the cart?
- Does Sliding Cart work (if enabled)?
- Can you empty the cart?
- Can you proceed to Checkout?
- If required, can customers register for an account on your store?
- Is tax automatically added?
- If you switch states or countries, are tax settings still appropriate?
- Are shipping settings calculated correctly?
- What about shipping for international orders?
- Is your payment gateway functioning?
- Is the payment gateway also receiving tax + shipping information?

Try to break the store:

- Can you check out without paying?
- Can you access a digital download without paying?
- Add an exorbitant amount of items to the cart. Does it still work?
- Try to gain access to an administrator's account. Can you?

If you do not try to break the store, rest assured that someone else will. Even though you're still operating on the testing server, it is imperative to know that everything works as planned. If all of the items in this checklist work as expected, without any problems, then you can feel fairly certain that everything will work when the site goes live. Once we release your site to the public, you must remember to go through this checklist again.

E-mails sent to the customer

Now is a good time to revisit the **E-mail Settings** that we discussed in Chapter 3, *Configure Your e-Commerce Settings*. In light of all the development that you have made on your site since that chapter, does the information that you are sending to the customer after each purchase still make sense? More importantly, are the e-mails actually being sent, or at least displayed to the customer on the Transaction Results page?

Depending on which payment gateway is used, the customer will likely also receive a payment notification directly from that gateway. If you are using a sandbox testing environment for your payment gateway (and you *should*), you can see how those e-mails will look by logging into the testing sandbox account. For example, you can check e-mail in the PayPal sandbox environment by clicking on the **Test Email** link once you have logged in:

When you complete a test purchase in the sandbox, your customer account should receive an e-mail similar to the one shown in the following screenshot:

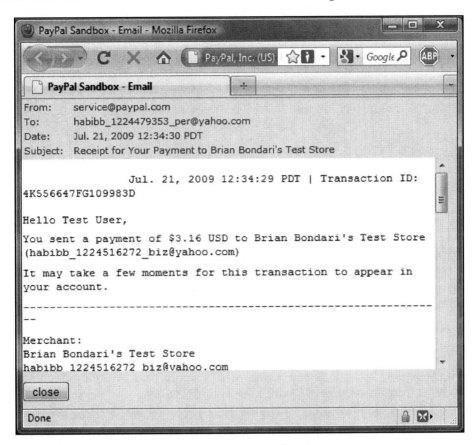

E-mails sent to you

After each purchase, you, as the store owner, should also receive a notification detailing the information about the order. The title of the e-mail will be **Purchase Report**, and it will be sent to the e-mail address that you designate next to Purchase Log Email in the Admin settings for your store. Once your store goes live, it's a good idea to log into your payment gateway to verify the accuracy of orders, at least for the first few months.

Sales log

Back on the Sales page for the WP e-Commerce plugin, you will find a *sales* log with details about purchases made so far. The sales log does not distinguish between test purchases made via a payment gateway sandbox and real transactions in which money was exchanged, so even if you have not made any legitimate sales on your site, you can still see how they *will* appear in your sales log, as shown in the following screenshot:

Here we have two sample transactions. The sales log displays for us the transaction date, the contact information for the buyer, the total amount, the number of items included, and the status of the order. To see the full information about the order, including the customer address, click on the link underneath the word **Details**.

Notice that the status is different for the two orders in this example. One has a status of **Order Received**, and the other reads **Closed Order**.

If you use Manual Payment as one of your payment gateway options, all incoming orders will default to a status of Order Received. This is because the Manual Payment gateway lacks the ability to automatically record a customer's payment and cannot know whether or not the transaction is actually complete. Therefore, it puts the responsibility on your shoulders to determine when to complete the order.

Manual Payment is useful if you offer the ability to accept personal checks or money orders. When the customer sends in the payment, it is up to you to ship the product and manually change the status of the order. You can do this by clicking on the drop-down menu under **Status**:

Payment gateways such as PayPal (with IPN) will automatically verify that a payment is complete and record the order in the sales log with a status of *closed*. If you somehow receive an order using a payment gateway that lacks *closed* status, be sure to verify that you have actually received payment before shipping the order.

Summary

Having a solid grasp of how you want to handle taxes and shipping is a major step toward the successful launch of your online store. After completing this chapter, you should know exactly how to implement a broad number of shipping modules and be able to determine which one(s) to integrate.

The following topics were covered in this chapter:

- Locations and tax setup—setting your correct home base location and charging appropriate taxes
- Shipping Options and Calculators—an overview of all five included shipping modules and how to use them
- Processing a test order—a detailed checklist of tasks to complete to gauge whether or not your sites works as expected
- E-mails sent to you and the customer—a revisit of some critical information regarding communication about purchases
- Sales log—a centralized location for tracking orders and their statuses

At this point, your store checkout process should include a functioning payment gateway that automatically includes and receives any additional costs for taxes and shipping. Your work is not yet complete, however. You still have to shift from the testing server to a production site and test some more before you know everything works thoroughly.

Remember that it is imperative to test every aspect of the checkout process before you can rest assured that it works. Use the checklist from this chapter to help guide you, but remember to go through it again and again once you upload your site to a production server.

Up next, we'll shift our focus from the purely functional to the cosmetic by exploring some layout and design issues.

Themes and Design Elements

8

In Chapter 2, *Getting Ready to Sell* we briefly discussed a few visual elements of a new WordPress installation, such as installing new themes and toying around with widgets. Now it's time to dig a little deeper into customizing the look and feel of your shop. Dealing with your online store's layout and design can simultaneously be a satisfying and maddeningly frustrating experience. Fortunately, you don't need to be a full-time designer or programmer in order to achieve a functional and tasteful look for your store-front, nor is there an absolute necessity to hire a designer to skin your shop.

If you do possess competent design skills, WordPress allows for full customization of existing themes or even construction of your own theme from scratch. If you are not comfortable with such a drastic undertaking, rest assured that there are a growing number of third-party themes either compatible with or designed especially for WP e-Commerce, and we can still achieve satisfactory design results by using the built-in tools that the plugin offers.

This chapter will cover:

- WP e-Commerce included widgets
- Shortcode and PHP tags
- WP e-Commerce theme engine
- Tweaking your WordPress theme

WP e-Commerce included widgets

The WP e-Commerce plugin comes bundled with numerous widgets that can help you further customize your shop and advertise your products.

They include:

- Latest Products
- Price Range
- Product Donations
- Product Tags
- Product Categories
- Product Specials
- Shopping Cart

Depending on your theme, you may have multiple sidebars or other locations in which to place widgets. To view all of your available widgets and possible locations, navigate to **Widgets** under **Appearance** in your WordPress menu, as seen below.

Just like with any other widgets for WordPress, you can drag and drop one or more widgets anywhere that your theme will allow. Each of them offers a dynamically changing element that serves a specific purpose.

Latest Products widget

Here is a good way to keep your customers informed of the newest additions to your store. If you add the *Latest Products* widget, your visitors will see a constantly updated list of your five most recently added items. If you associate an image with a product, it will display as a thumbnail.

By default, the widget heading will be **Latest Products**, but you can change it if desired. We will call ours **Newest Items**, as seen in the image below.

Price Range widget

As the name implies, the *Price Range* widget can help your customers search for products that fall within certain price ranges. Currently, there is no ability to customize the given price ranges, but perhaps this feature will become available in a future release.

For most shop owners, though, the default ranges should work nicely. There are four zones given by default, ranging from **Under 10** to **Over 100**:

Price Range
Under 10
10 - 20
20 - 100
Over 100
Show All

Clicking on one of the zones will only display products that fit into that price range.

Product Donations widget

As you might suspect, the *Product Donations* widget provides a convenient way for your customers to *purchase* a donation. If that sounds confusing, it shouldn't. The WP e-Commerce plugin treats donations like any other product that you might offer to your customers. Notice that the widget is called "Product Donations" and not just "Donations".

When you add this widget to your shop, don't be surprised if it appears not to work. This is because the widget only gets its input from products that you have specifically flagged as *donation* products. You can do this in your Product Catalog. When editing the attributes for an individual product, look for the checkbox under **Price and Stock Control** that reads, **This is a donation**, as shown in the following screenshot:

Price and Stock Control
☐ Do not include tax (tax is set in shop config)
☑ This is a donation (only show it in the donations widget)
☐ Table Rate Price
☐ Custom Tax Rate
☐ I have a limited number of this item in stock. If the stock runs out, this product will not be available on the shop unless you untick this box or add more stock.

Once that option is selected, only then will that product appear wherever you place the *Product Donations* widget. An ideal use for this feature is to allow customers to set their own price for a product. For instance, a shop owner selling digital MP3 audio files or photography could occasionally release a new file as a donation, allowing customers to pay what they think it is worth. An example of this can be seen in the following screenshot:

Product Tags widget

Perhaps you have visited websites or blogs that utilize a *tag cloud* (sometimes called a *word cloud*), which is a popular way of visually depicting the content of a site using user-generated tags. Arranged alphabetically, the relative size of the tag shows its importance or frequency of occurrence. In other words, the more frequently a tag is associated with an item, the greater weight it will have, resulting in a larger appearance within the cloud.

By using the *Product Tags* widget, we can do the same thing using tags that we have associated with our items. Here is a basic example:

A tag cloud serves a functional as well as a visual purpose. Clicking on an individual tag will display all of the products associated with it. Of course, you must have tags associated with your individual items for it to work properly. When adding or editing an item, look for the **Product Tags** section under the **Categories and Tags** heading, as seen below.

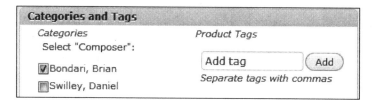

You can add as many tags as you like, separated by commas.

Product Categories widget

As expected, the *Product Categories* widget displays a list of the categories that host your products. Keep in mind that these are different from the *Posts* categories that WordPress uses.

For the widget to work properly, you must select one or more of your Groups to display, as seen below.

If you wish, you can use more than one Product Categories widget. For our music shop, we can display one widget for **Composers** and another widget for **Genres**, with the widget titles changed accordingly, as seen below.

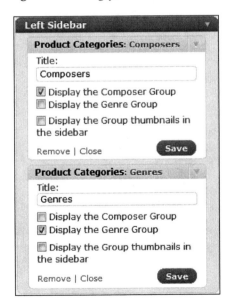

Product Specials widget

Need a place to highlight your *on-sale* items? You can use the *Product Specials* widget to ensure that your customers won't miss your discounted items. Just like with the *Product Donations* widget, you must first flag certain items as being "on sale" for the widget to receive input from them.

You can do this by setting a **Sale Price** when editing one or more of your products in your catalog, as seen in the screenshot below.

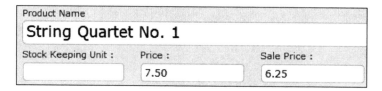

Products with automatic discounts will appear wherever you place the *Product Specials* widget, thereby garnering customer attention.

Shopping Cart widget

This last widget is self-explanatory. If you want to ensure that your shopping cart is always visible across your store, even when empty, you can utilize the *Shopping Cart* widget.

One nice advantage of using this widget is that the empty cart displays an added link to your products page, giving first-time customers an additional way to quickly find your items for sale. The widget will display like this:

Shortcode and PHP tags

Shortcode and PHP tags are advanced means of customizing your online store. Using literally a short snippet of code, you can add any number of functional bits to your store. These can:

- Display default products
- Display shopping cart
- List categories

- Display products from a specific group
- Buy now
- Add to cart

So, what is the difference between a shortcode and a PHP tag? From a visual standpoint, a shortcode is a snippet of text between square brackets, such as this: [dosomething]. In a nutshell, a shortcode is really just a macro code that can be expanded at runtime to reflect some dynamic contents. WordPress started supporting shortcode as of version 2.5, and many plugins now take advantage of it, allowing end users to gain functionality without the need to dig into any complex HTML or embedded codes.

On the other hand, PHP code tags harness the power and versatility of the PHP scripting language to perform a specified action or display some content. Visually, it looks like this:

```
<?php do_something(); ?>
```

The above code shows the opening (<?php) and closing (?>) tag elements, as well as a function in the middle that performs a certain task. That task will naturally vary depending upon the function.

The functional tasks that shortcode and PHP tags can perform are duplicated by each other in many cases. That is, the same task can be performed by either a shortcode or a PHP tag. The difference lies in where you want that function to execute: *PHP tags are placed directly in your WordPress theme, whereas shortcode are placed in posts or pages.*

Display default products

If you want to display a list of products inherited from your default category, you may do so in any post or page by adding the following shortcode:

Code: [productspage]

Display shopping cart

If you need full control over the location of your shopping cart, use the PHP tag given below, which will display your cart wherever you place it within your theme. Typical locations include within the theme sidebar or header.

Code: `<?php echo nzshpcrt_shopping_basket(); ?>`

List categories

By using this tag, you can display a list of your product categories, including thumbnail images. You can use either a shortcode or a PHP tag, as shown below, respectively:

Code: `[showcategories]`

Code: `<?php show_cats_brands(); ?>`

Display products from a specific group

It's easy to show a list of products within a specific group. We don't even have to memorize a given shortcode, since they are all generated automatically for us. To display all products from a specific group, first navigate to your **Categories** page under the **Products** menu, then click on the **Edit** button next to your desired Group. To the right-hand side, you should see all of the attributes for that Group, as well as the custom shortcode and PHP tags, as seen below.

You are editing an item in the "Composer" Group
You are editing the "Bondari, Brian" Group
+ Add new category to the current Group
Display Category Shortcode:
`[wpsc_products category_url_name='bondari-brian']`
Display Category Template Tag:
`<?php echo wpsc_display_products(array('category_url_name'=>'bondari-brian')); ?>`

In the previous example, we would use the **[wpsc_products category_url_ name='bondari-brian']** shortcode to display all items in that Group. There's also a corresponding PHP tag.

Add to Cart / Buy Now

Want full control over placing individual products in your posts, pages, or theme? Don't worry, there are shortcode and PHP tags for that, too.

An **Add to Cart** or **Buy Now** button *must* also have a corresponding product tag in order to work correctly.

The easiest way to find all the code required for individual products is to navigate back to your product catalog and select your desired product. When editing that product, you should notice the blue information icon to the right-hand side of the product name, as seen below.

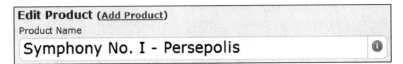

By clicking on the information icon, you will expose a plethora of code and tags unique to that product, as seen below.

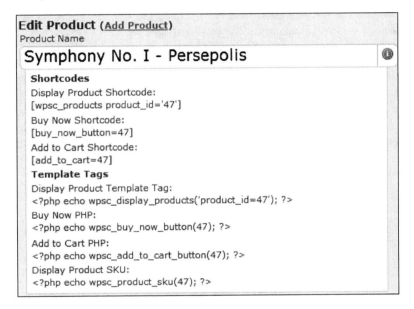

All we have to do is copy and paste the text snippets to our desired post, page, or theme location. Keep in mind that an "Add to Cart" or "Buy Now" button cannot exist without an associated product, so don't forget the product shortcode or tag.

The "Buy Now" option bypasses the shopping cart, but only works with either Google Checkout or PayPal Express. Stick to the "Add to Cart" code for other payment gateways.

WP e-Commerce theme engine

As of version 3.6.9 of the WP e-Commerce plugin, a theme engine is now available. What does this mean? Developers rejoice! You can now create your own themes directly for WP e-Commerce.

 Keep in mind that these themes differ from regular WordPress themes. They are unique to the e-Commerce plugin.

So, what is meant by a WP e-Commerce theme? These refer to the themes that you can select specifically for your shop. Three of them come bundled with the plugin: the *Default* theme, the *iShop* theme, and the *Marketplace* theme. You can switch between them in your **e-Commerce Presentation** settings.

Upon a fresh installation, all your e-Commerce theme files will reside in your `wp-content/plugins/wp-e-commerce/themes/` directory. If you have not already done so, one of the first things you should do is move those files to a safer location. The problem is that because those files live in your `wp-e-commerce` directory, any changes or customizations that you make to your themes will be overwritten the next time you upgrade the plugin. In fact, the plugin developers disable the automatic upgrade for WP e-Commerce installations that have not yet moved those theme files to a place where they will not get overwritten.

In your **Presentation** settings, you should see a warning about your themes if you have not yet moved them, as shown in the following screenshot:

Theme Customisation
Your theme files have not been moved.
Until your theme files have been moved, we have disabled automatic upgrades.
Click here to Move your files to a safe place
Read Tutorials

Fortunately, the plugin can move the files for you. All you have to do is follow the **Move your files** prompt if you see the warning. If you need to move the theme files manually for some reason, the correct destination is `wp-content/uploads/wpsc/themes`.

Creating a new e-Commerce theme

Once you have backed up your theme files to the appropriate place, you can work on creating a new theme. The easiest way to get started with a new theme is to make a full backup of the **default** theme folder inside `wp-content/uploads/wpsc/themes`. Once you have a backup copy:

1. Give the folder a new name, such as `myshoptheme`.

2. Inside that folder, you will find a file called `default.css`. Rename that file to the same name as the containing folder. In our case, we will change the name to `myshoptheme.css`. The names must match.

3. Open `myshoptheme.css` in your favorite text editor. At the top of the file, you will find the existing theme name and other relevant information. Change it as you desire. Keep in mind that the **Theme Name** that you enter is what will be displayed when selecting that theme in your **e-Commerce Presentation** settings. Below is an example.

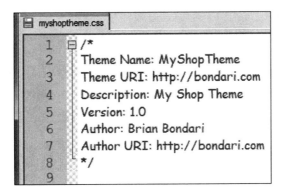

For now, go ahead and save the file. When you navigate to your e-Commerce Presentation settings and click on the drop-down list next to **Select Theme**, you should see your newly created theme as an option, as shown below.

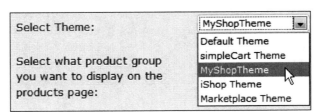

Of course, your new theme is currently nothing but an exact duplicate of the **Default Theme**. If you're comfortable with HTML, PHP, and CSS, you are now in a terrific position to modify the theme to your heart's content. We'll discuss some code basics in the following section, but for the time being, feast your eyes on the skeletal structure of your new theme files.

File/Folder Name	Contents
Images (folder)	Contains all images related to your theme, such as "Add to Cart" and "Buy Now" buttons.
cart_widget.php	Contains scripts and markup related to the shopping cart widget.
category_widget.php	Contains code related to the category widget.
functions.php	Controls your theme pagination settings.
grid_view.php	Relevant only for people who have purchased the Gold Cart, this file contains markup related to the Grid View layout option.
list_view.php	Contains code related to categories and display of products.
your_shop_theme.css	Contains all the gory details pertaining to the layout of your shop (this is the file that we renamed earlier).
products_page.php	Contains code related to your main products page.
shopping_cart_page.php	Contains all the code for your checkout page.
single_product.php	Contains code for displaying single product pages.

You are welcome to modify any and all of these files. If this task seems beyond your development skills, don't fret. Let's move away from e-Commerce themes for the time being and focus instead on making tweaks to themes for WordPress.

Tweaking your WordPress theme

A quick scouring of the Web reveals that there are literally thousands of themes available for WordPress. The sheer amount of choice that we have is great. It also means that we do not have to know how to build an entire theme from scratch just to have some semblance of a unique theme. Still, we *can* build entire WordPress themes from scratch, and if you are interested in learning how to do so, we suggest reading the latest edition of *WordPress Theme Design* (ISBN: 978-1-849510-08-0).

Many shop owners are perfectly happy using freely available third-party themes without making any adjustments at all. The downside to this approach is that there are bound to be dozens, or even hundreds, of other sites out there that look almost exactly like your shop. You can easily boost the originality factor of your store by learning a few basic tweaks. In most cases, the adjustments are simple, such as:

- Changing the header image on a theme you love.
- Replacing the fonts included in the theme.
- Adjusting colors in a theme with a good layout.

These three basic tweaks—changing the header image, replacing fonts, and adjusting colors, can have a tremendous visual impact on your theme. Fortunately, they are all easy to do. Before you begin, it's a good idea to make a backup of your theme folder. That way, you can revert to a fresh starting place in case some of your tweaks go awry.

CSS basics

A **Cascading Style Sheet (CSS)** influences every WordPress theme you have ever used. It is unequivocally the heart and soul of your theme design. In days long-gone-by, creating any major alterations to a website's design required a direct modification of the markup language (HTML). With CSS, you can control how the text and layout look for the entire site just by altering a single file. We cannot significantly discuss our site's look and feel without involving CSS, so it is prudent to learn a few of the basics.

When someone browses your online store, the CSS for your WordPress theme is loaded through the Header template (`header.php`) and is called `style.css`.

 For the purposes of this tutorial, we will focus on the WordPress Default theme, though almost any theme should be similar.

Go to your WordPress Dashboard and click on the **Editor** link underneath the **Appearance** menu, as seen below.

In the right-hand side column of the Theme Editor, take a look at the file called Header (`header.php`). Part-way down the page, you should see a line of code like this:

```
<link rel="stylesheet" href="<?php bloginfo('stylesheet_url'); ?>"
type="text/css" media="screen" />
```

What this seemingly innocuous line of code does is pull the style sheet into the page, thereby loading all the formatting elements for your entire site. Be careful not to edit that code, or you risk losing all of your site's formatting, giving it a disturbingly spartan look! On the other hand, if you wish to behold the power of CSS, cut that little bit of code from your theme and then save the file. Try loading your site, but do your best to stifle your scream when viewing the horror of your un-formatted shop. That is the power of CSS in action. Needless to say, be sure to replace that code snippet before continuing.

CSS selectors

CSS allows you to add style and flair (such as size, color, and specific placement) to the elements of your site. You can do this using a basic syntax comprised of three parts: the selector, the property, and the value:

```
selector {property:value;}
```

CSS selectors contain the properties and values that define the HTML elements/tags that you wish to style. Here are some examples of CSS selectors:

Basic CSS selectors

CSS selector	Description	HTML	CSS code
body	Controls the style of the body for your site, such as the page background color and the default fonts	`<body>lots of content</body>`	`body {background-color:white;}` Makes the background color for all pages white
p	Controls the formatting for paragraphs	`<p>some text</p>`	`p {color:black;}` Makes all the text used in paragraphs black

h1, h2, h3, h4	Controls the style for section headings	`<h1>Section Title</h1>`	`h1`
			
			`{`
			
			`font-size:20pt;`
			
			`text-align:right;`
			
			`}`
			
			All the text surrounded by `<h1>` tags will be size 20pt and aligned to the right

a	Affects the styling of hyperlinks on your site	`<a href="http://your-link.com">Link Text</a>`	`a {color:green;}` All links on your site will be green

Class and ID selectors

If you take a look at the stylesheet (`style.css`) that comes with the WordPress Default theme, a lot of it may look overwhelming. As you scroll down the page, do you notice how many of the elements begin either with a hash mark (#) or a period? Here are two examples:

- **#page** — since it begins with a hash mark, this is called a CSS ID.
- **.widecolumn** — since it begins with a period, this is called a CSS Class.

Both classes and IDs contain styling attributes, but they control different sections of your site. For example, let's say that we want to create two types of paragraph styles for our site: one that is centered and one that is aligned to the right. We can easily do that using a *class*, as seen below.

```
.center {text-align:center;}
.right {text-align:right;}
```

When writing our code, all we have to do now is refer to the appropriate class within our paragraph tags, as such:

```
<p class="center">The text in this paragraph will be centered."</p>
<p class="right">The text in this paragraph will be aligned to the right.</p>
```

A CSS ID functions similarly, but the selector is called using an ID attribute. In its most basic form, such an example might look like this:

```
#blue {color:blue;}
```

And now, to reference it:

```
<p id="blue">This text will display with a blue color.</p>
```

With this knowledge, we can more easily understand the general styling areas of our theme, and we can figure out where to look if we want to customize a certain area.

When CSS selectors meet HTML

CSS selector	HTML	Description
#page	`<div id="page">`	Controls the styling for the *page* element within your template. In this case, the ID name is *page*.
#header	`<div id="header">`	Controls the styling for the *header* ID.
#headerimg	`<div id="headerimg">`	Controls the styling for the *headerimg* ID.
#footer	`<div id="footer">`	Controls the styling for the *footer* ID.
.post	`<div class="post">`	Controls the styling for the *post* class.

So, when should you use a class versus an ID? A general rule is that you should stick to classes for multiple occurrences on a single page, and rely on IDs for single occurrences on a page.

If nothing else, keep in mind that if you see a reference to an ID (such as `div id=` or `p id=`, look for the corresponding hash mark (#) in the stylesheet. If you see a reference to a class (such as `div class=` or `p class=`, look for the corresponding period in the stylesheet next to the class name.

CSS properties and values

Each CSS Selector has a corresponding property, and each contains a value. Remember that the basic syntax is:

```
selector {property:value;}
```

Let's examine the following example:

```
#page {
    background-color:yellow;
    border: 1px solid #959596;
    text-align:left;
    }
```

First of all, notice how the indents make this CSS easier to understand than if it were one long line of text.

Secondly, the CSS selector in the above example is page, which has three properties.

- `background-color`, which has a value of `yellow`.
- `border`, which has the value `1px solid #959596`. These elements describe the border thickness, style, and specific color, respectively.
- `text-align`, which is positioned to the `left`.

When properties are used, each property is followed by a colon (`:`), and each value is followed by a semicolon (`;`). Here are some commonly used CSS properties and values:

Frequently used CSS properties and values

Property	Value	Example CSS
background	Sets all the background parameters in one fell swoop	```body {``` ```background: #00ff00 url('image.gif') no-repeat fixed center;``` ```}```
background-color	Sets the color of the background, such as white, red, or green	```#page {``` ```background-color:white;``` ```}```
background-image	Sets the background image for an element	```body {``` ```background-image:url('your-image.gif');``` ```}```
color	Sets the color of the text	```h3 {``` ```color:blue;``` ```}```

Frequently used CSS properties and values

Property	Value	Example CSS

font-family	Specifies the font family for the selector	```p {```
		
		```font-family:"Times New Roman", Veranda, Arial, Serif;```
		
		```}```
		
		Use quotes for font names that include a space

font-size	Specifies the size of a font	```h1 {```
		
		```font-size:200%;```
		
		```}```

text-align	Sets the alignment of the text	```p {```
		
		```text-align:center;```
		
		```}```

Changing the header image

Almost every theme has some kind of image in the header. Generally, replacing that image with one of your own choosing is relatively simple. A few themes even come with their own user-friendly options for replacing the header image, but if your theme does not, you can still customize it.

The header image is loaded from a graphic file defined in the CSS property for the header area. Use the WordPress Default theme as an example. If you open the Header file (`header.php`), you can find the markup for the header image, listed below:

```
<div id="header" role="banner">
    <div id="headerimg">
        <h1><a href="<?php echo get_option('home'); ?>/"><?php
bloginfo('name'); ?></a></h1>
        <div class="description"><?php bloginfo('description'); ?></div>
    </div>
</div>
```

What does it all mean?

- `<div id="header" role="banner">`

  This line corresponds with the `#header` ID selector in your stylesheet. In order to change the image, edit the name of the file in the *background* property of the #header ID.

- `<div id="headerimg">`

  This line corresponds to the `#headerimg` selector in your stylesheet. It controls such aspects as the height, width, and margins of the header image.

- `<h1><a href="<?php echo get_option('home'); ?>/"><?php bloginfo('name'); ?></a></h1>`

  This line displays the name of your WordPress site as specified in your Admin settings. The `<a>` HTML tag links it to your homepage. All of it is wrapped inside an `<h1>` tag, which inherits its properties from the `h1` selector in your stylesheet.

- `<div class="description"><?php bloginfo('description'); ?></div>`

  This line corresponds with the `.description` selector in your stylesheet. It contains your WordPress site's description or tagline (that is, *Just another WordPress weblog*).

- `</div>`

  This snippet closes the opening `<div id="headerimg">` markup.

- `</div>`

  And this snippet closes the opening `<div id="header">` markup. Remember that once you open a `<div>` tag, it must have a respective closing tag.

To actually replace the header image, all we need to do is upload our new image and then change the image name in the CSS. To do so:

1. Using your preferred FTP program, upload your new image to the images folder for your theme. If you are using the Default theme, the path is: `wp-content/themes/default/images/`. Let's assume that your new header image is called `new-image.jpg`.

2. In your WordPress Dashboard, go to the Theme Editor (under the *Appearance* menu). Be sure to select the correct theme from the drop-down menu, shown below.

3. Open your theme's main stylesheet, usually called `style.css`.

4. Scroll down the page until you find the `#header` selector. In the WordPress Default theme, it looks like this:

```
#header {
    background: #73a0c5 url('images/kubrickheader.jpg') no-repeat
bottom center;
    }
```

5. Change the background property's value to reflect the new name of your uploaded image. In our case, we specifically change the URL section to `url('images/new-image.jpg')`.

6. Save your modified CSS by clicking on the **Update File** button at the bottom of the page. When you visit your site, you should see your updated header image!

Replacing the theme fonts

As you've seen, CSS is quite powerful, and minor tweaks can have big impacts. If you are unhappy with the fonts used in your WordPress theme, adjusting them all is easy. Fonts come in all shapes and sizes, and a font change can alter your site's look and feel dramatically.

Keep in mind that not all fonts display properly in all browsers. To compensate, you can designate *fallback* fonts. If a user's browser cannot render the desired font, it will try the next in line. To be safe, it is important to know that individual fonts come in generic families. All the fonts in a generic family share a similar look:

Generic family	Some individual fonts	General description
Sans-Serif	Arial, Tahoma, Trebuchet MS, Veranda	Sans-Serif fonts lack the lines and character markings that Serif fonts have.
Serif	Bookman Old Style, Garamond, Georgia, Times New Roman	Serif fonts contain small lines and markings on the ends of certain characters.
Monospace	Consolas, Courier New, Lucida Console, Monaco	The characters in Monospace fonts all have the same width.

In order to change the font(s) used in your theme, you need to open your stylesheet (`style.css`). Find the section that looks like this:

```
body {
    font-size: 62.5%; /* Resets 1em to 10px */
    font-family: 'Lucida Grande', Verdana, Arial, Sans-Serif;
    background: #d5d6d7 url('images/kubrickbgcolor.jpg');
    color: #333;
    text-align: center;
    }
```

You can change the size of your font by adjusting the value of the `font-size` property. In the WordPress Default theme, the font-size value is listed as a percentage (`62.5%`). There are several ways that we can describe font sizes, three of which we list here:

1. **In Points** — increasing or decreasing the number of points changes the size of the font, such as `12pt` (higher is larger, naturally). This is similar to adjusting font size in a word processing program.

2. **In Pixels** — if you want ultimate control over the font size, you can set it in number of pixels, such as `14px` (higher is larger, naturally). There's just one problem: this method has been known not to work with Internet Explorer, though it does work in other mainstream browsers.

3. **As a Percentage** — raising or lowering the percentage number changes the font size accordingly. 100% is equivalent to 17px.

If you want to replace the default fonts, you can do so by adjusting the value of the `font-family` property. Our example begins with specific fonts (Lucida Grande) and ends with a generic font family (Sans-Serif). A user's web browser will try the fonts in order, and if the first listed font will not display properly, it will move to the second, and so on, until it finally reaches the generic font family. Beginning designers quickly realize that design is a game of compromise — it is virtually impossible to code in such a way that all users see exactly the same thing. That said, it's better to give the browser a slight influence (in this case, by suggesting a font family) rather than leaving everything up to chance.

Our last font element is the `color` property. You can replace the default value (`#333`) with any color that you like. We will learn more about colors in the next section.

At this point, you should be comfortable with the idea of replacing fonts. Feel free to sift through the various other elements of your stylesheet in search of fonts that you wish to adjust, such as the fonts used in your heading tags.

Changing the theme colors

This brings us to our last bit of tweaking: the colors used in our theme. Let's examine that style used for the text body in your stylesheet once again:

```
body {
    font-size: 62.5%; /* Resets 1em to 10px */
    font-family: 'Lucida Grande', Verdana, Arial, Sans-Serif;
    background: #d5d6d7 url('images/kubrickbgcolor.jpg');
    color: #333;
    text-align: center;
    }
```

Take a look at the value given for the `background` property. Notice how it has both a color and an image? We can use a combination of colors and images when styling our theme.

- **Colors** — unless you are satisfied with a generic color (white, black, red, and so on), you can pinpoint a specific hue by using its representative hexadecimal (*hex* for short) code. Hex codes begin with a hash mark (#) followed by six numbers or letters. The given hex code in this example is `#d5d6d7`. Many great resources for hex codes abound on the Internet. One particularly good one can be found at `http://www.w3schools.com/Html/html_colornames.asp`.

- **Images** — you can also use an image as a background by uploading it to the images folder in your theme directory and altering the link to the correct name. The format would be: `background: url('images/your-image-name.jpg')`. Keep in mind that the `url` element pulls in your domain name, so there is no need to add the full URL to the image.

Let's change a couple of colors in our theme, starting with the background color.

1. In your WordPress Dashboard, go to the **Theme Editor** (under the **Appearance** menu). Be sure to select the correct theme from the drop-down menu.

2. Open your theme's main stylesheet, usually called `style.css`.

3. Scroll down to the body section of the stylesheet. It's just underneath a comment that reads `/* Begin Typography & Colors */`.

4. Change the line that reads:

   ```
   background: #d5d6d7 url('images/kubrickbgcolor.jpg');
   ```

   to this:

   ```
   background: grey;
   ```

5. Of course, you can use any generic color or hex code that you like. Once you have made your choice, click on the **Update File** button to save your changes. When you visit your site, you can view your new background color.

You can repeat this process for other sections of your site. For instance, if you want to adjust the color of your site footer, just scroll down to the #footer ID in your stylesheet and adjust the properties.

Additional CSS tutorials

We have only scratched the surface of what you can do using CSS. It's beyond the scope of this book to delve further into CSS styling, but if we have piqued your interest, here are a few resources on the Internet that you can investigate:

* http://www.w3schools.com/css/
* http://www.csstutorial.net/
* http://www.westciv.com/courses/

Additional WP e-Commerce themes

We covered the installation of third-party themes back in Chapter 2, *Getting Ready to Sell* but it is fair to mention that there is a growing collection of themes designed especially with the WP e-Commerce plugin in mind. Many of these themes are free, though some are commercial only.

You can view and download these themes here:
http://www.getshopped.org/extend/themes

WP e-Commerce tips

We have covered a lot of ground in this chapter, but before we bring it to a close, here are a handful of extra tips that will help you personalize your site and (hopefully) make it more aesthetically pleasing. These final tips only scratch the surface of what is possible, but should get you started in creating further customizations. For all of these tips, you will make your modifications to either an existing theme or a theme of your own creation inside the wp-content/uploads/wpsc/themes folder:

* Change the appearance of the shopping cart widget
* Use a custom Add to Cart image
* Remove the sidebar Google Checkout button

Change the appearance of the shopping cart widget

Most shop owners are likely to run their shopping carts as a sidebar widget. Those who do will notice that the shopping cart is more functional than flashy. However, the shopping cart is easy to style using a few CSS tweaks.

To do so, open the stylesheet for your particular WP e-Commerce theme. Keep in mind that this is not your regular WordPress theme, but the theme file inside your `wp-content/uploads/wpsc/themes` folder. For instance, if you are using the iShop theme, your stylesheet will be called `iShop.css`.

Inside the stylesheet, find the section that looks like this:

```
div#sliding_cart{
margin: 0px;
padding: 0px;
background: none;
border: none;
}
```

This is the CSS that controls how the sidebar shopping cart looks, and right now it has essentially no styling. Depending upon your WordPress theme, your cart might look something like this:

Your Cart
Number of items: 1

Product	Qty	Price
Sample CD	1	$5.00
Shipping:		$2.00
Tax:		$0.25
Total:		$7.25

Empty your cart
Go to Checkout

Rather spartan, isn't it? Using some of the CSS knowledge gleaned from this chapter, you can easily make a few minor adjustments to the way the cart looks.

You can add a little padding, change the font color, make the font a bit larger, and add a dashed border all around the shopping cart:

```
div#sliding_cart{
   margin: 0px;
   padding: 5px;
   background: none;
  color: #330066;
   border: 1px dashed #000000;
   font-size: 12px;
   }
```

When you save the file and refresh the page, you should see something like this:

It's not much, but it's a slight improvement. The possibilities are endless, so feel free to experiment.

Use a custom Add to Cart image

Here is a handy tip to make your store look a little more unique: use your own *Add to Cart* button. This is incredibly easy to do if you already use the iShop theme, but any other e-Commerce theme will work.

 For simplicity's sake, we recommend using the iShop theme, or a copy of it, as the starting point for this tip.

First, open the stylesheet for your theme, just as in the previous tip. Next, scroll down until you see the following code:

```
input.wpsc_buy_button{
  background-image: url(images/buy_button.gif);
  border: none;
  width: 76px;
```

```
height: 25px;
text-align: center;
/*  vertical-align: top; */
padding: 0px 0px 0px 0px;
font-size: 8pt;
margin-top: 3px;
color: #6a6c74;
}
```

This is the code that controls how the *Add to Cart* button appears, taken directly from the `iShop.css` file. If you are using the Default or the Marketplace theme as your foundation, you will not see this much styling. In particular, notice how this section contains a `background-image` with a `url` associated with it. That is the image that currently displays as your *Add to Cart* button.

Using your own image takes only a few steps. First, browse to `wp-content/uploads/wpsc/themes/<theme name>/images/`. Replace `<theme name>` with whichever theme you are using, such as iShop. Notice that in this folder there is an image called **buy_button.gif**, as seen below.

4 Directories and Files (0 Selected)	Refresh List	
Filename ▲		**Size**
📁 [Parent Directory]		
🖼 buy_button.gif		1.93 KB
🖼 iShop_search.png		1.2 KB
🖼 itembg.gif		1.26 KB
🖼 old-buy_button.gif		1.46 KB

Here, you need to give your new image that same name and upload it to this folder, replacing the original. You may also rename the original and keep it as a backup. Also, it is safest to go ahead and upload that same replacement image to `wp-content/plugins/wp-e-commerce/themes/<theme name>/images/`. If you do not, you may run into a frustrating problem in which no matter how many times you refresh the page on your online store, the *Add to Cart* image does not update. This is because (as of this writing) the `url` for the CSS `background-image` is still referencing the latter path. You can correct this problem by updating the `url` to the absolute path on your server.

 The absolute path is not a URL, but the file system path on your web server. This will path will differ depending on your web host. If in doubt, see your host's documentation or contact them directly.

The final step is to modify the width and height in the CSS to the appropriate values for your new image. You can find the width and height in pixels for your image by opening it in a program such as Photoshop, GIMP, or Paint.net.

If you have done everything correctly, you should see your new image next to each product on your site. You can see a different *Add to Cart* button in the following screenshot:

Remove the sidebar Google Checkout button

Here's a tip that you might find helpful. If you use Google Checkout as one of your payment gateways, you will notice that an extra Google Checkout button may appear in your WordPress sidebar once you add an item to your shopping cart. Some people may like this "extra" button, but others may want their customers to proceed to the regular check out before the button is displayed.

In any case, if you want to prevent that "extra" Google Checkout button from ever displaying, here is how to do it: Inside your preferred theme folder, you should see a file called `cart_widget.php` (example path: `wp-content/uploads/wpsc/themes/iShop/cart_widget.php`).

Open that file and scroll to the bottom. At or near the bottom you should see some text like this:

```
<?php
wpsc_google_checkout();
?>
```

That is the code that displays the Google Checkout button in the sidebar. If you wish, you may safely delete those lines. Another option is to comment out the middle line by adding two forward slashes:

```
<?php
// wpsc_google_checkout();
?>
```

That will prevent the "extra" Google Checkout button from displaying in the sidebar.

Summary

As you can see, you don't need to be a full-time designer in order to customize the look and feel of your shop. From drag-and-drop widgets to making CSS tweaks, there are a number of ways to improve the functionality and originality of our online stores.

This chapter covered:

- WP e-Commerce included widgets
- Shortcodes and PHP tags
- WP e-Commerce theme engine
- Tweaking your WordPress theme

By this point, hopefully you are comfortable with the visual elements of your shop. When you're ready, move on to the next chapter, which deals with some of the most important issues of all: site deployment, security, and maintenance issues.

Deploy, Secure, and Maintain Your Shop

9

At last, the time has come to officially launch your e-Commerce site. During this process, we will transfer our files from the testing platform to a production server, thereby potentially putting our products within reach of millions of customers. It's a big event, but we want to make sure that we do it right! There are numerous pitfalls that can occur along the way, so we want to make sure that we minimize those pitfalls.

Getting our site officially online opens another can of worms regarding site security. Dealing with potential security issues naturally reminds us of the need for data backups. We have a lot to cover, so let's get started.

This chapter covers:

- Getting ready to deploy
- Uploading your shop
- Man the hatches — essential site security
- Backups — preparing for disasters

Getting ready to deploy

The first thing we need to consider is the current state of our site. Are we happy with the way it looks and runs right now? Naturally, we can continue to make additional changes once the files have been transferred to the production server, but there's no need to complicate what is meant to be a straightforward process. If there are any remaining visual or functional tweaks, go ahead and complete them before uploading your site to the server.

Otherwise, there are only a few quick adjustments we need to make within WordPress before we can upload everything.

Necessary WordPress adjustments

There are only two slight changes to WordPress that you should make before you can continue the deployment:

1. Disable all WordPress plugins
2. Change the URL

The first step is to disable all plugins within WordPress. Yes, this includes the WP e-Commerce plugin. To do so, the quickest way is to browse to the Plugins section, select all of your plugins, and choose **Deactivate** from the **Bulk Actions** drop-down menu:

While deactivating all of your plugins is not a life-or-death requirement, it is standard practice when dealing with any WordPress transfers or updates. By doing so, you remove one variable from the "things that can go wrong" when setting up the new server. It's better to make sure your WordPress core is functioning properly before waking up the plugins, one by one.

Once this step is complete, we can move on to the remaining preparation involving WordPress: changing the URL. The basic idea here is that you need to change the URL required to access your WordPress site before you upload it to the server, lest you are unable to access it afterwards. This step is essential, although it is drastically more difficult, though not impossible, to alter the URL once the database and new files are in place on the new server.

To change the URL, navigate to **Settings | General** in the sidebar. If your testing platform is your personal computer, your current URL is probably something like *localhost* or *127.0.0.1*. We need to change this to the URL that we will use to access the site on the production server. So, whatever the domain name is that you have purchased, enter it in the fields for **WordPress address (URL)** and **Blog address (URL)**:

WordPress address (URL)	your URL here	
Blog address (URL)	your URL here	Enter
	the address here if you want your blog homepage to be different from the directory you installed WordPress.	

When you save your changes, don't be alarmed if your site stops responding. In fact, this is a good thing because it means that your URL has officially changed and your site can no longer be accessed at its former location. Just take a deep breath and accept that your site is out of your reach, for the moment.

Your WordPress database

As you probably recall from initially setting up WordPress, all of WordPress' settings are stored in a database. This database is invaluable because without it, not only will WordPress not work, but you will also have lost all of your posts, pages, and comments, as well as your WP e-Commerce products and settings. It's not enough to simply transfer your existing files and folders to your new server, but you must also export your database, import it on the production server, and then tell your transferred WordPress setup how to connect to the new database. It may sound like a lot of work, but it really is not.

At this point, let's talk about how to export and save your existing WordPress database. We'll cover importing in the next section. There are several ways to export a copy of your database. We'll cover two of them in this chapter: one graphical and one command-line method.

Database export via phpMyAdmin

Depending on who (or what) is hosting your testing platform, chances are pretty high that you have access to phpMyAdmin (one of the premiere graphical ways to access and administer MySQL databases). If you are using the WAMP testing platform, you already have access to phpMyAdmin.

If access to this tool is available, go ahead and launch it. Many hosts are different, but if you're confused, find the "databases" section of your host's control panel and look for a link called **Admin** next to your database (if in doubt, consult your host's documentation):

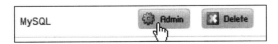

On the left-hand column within phpMyAdmin, click on the name of your database to make sure that it is the selected database. You should see your database name at the top of that column with a list of tables beneath it:

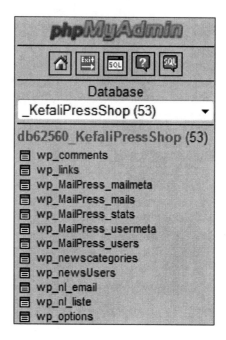

Now that you're inside your database, switch to the **Export** tab near the top of the page:

The **Export** page offers a plethora of options you might want to set for the database export. There's some flexibility involved, but most importantly, be sure to select all of the tables before you export the data. The following are some recommended settings:

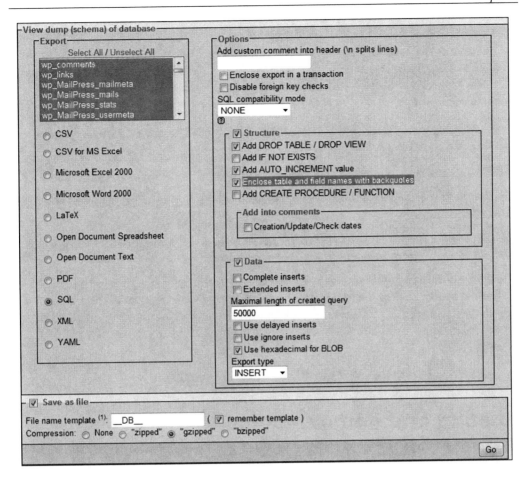

Under **Structure**, select:

- **Add DROP TABLE / DROP VIEW**
- **Add AUTO_INCREMENT value**
- **Enclose table and field names with backquotes**

Under **Data**, select:

- **Use hexadecimal for BLOB**

Under **Save as file**:

- Choose **"gzipped"** compression

Click on **Go** in order to export and download your database. Be sure to keep this file in a safe place as we will need it momentarily to import your database to the new server.

Database export via command line

If you have command line access to your (Linux) testing platform, you can perform a database backup in one fell swoop. This backup file is in no way different or better than one created via phpMyAdmin, but for people comfortable with a shell, it's much faster.

First, navigate to the directory that contains your WordPress files. This is where we will dump the database:

```
user@linux:~$ cd your-files/wordpress
```

Next, we will use the *mysqldump* tool to dump all of the tables in the database to a file. Here is an example:

```
user@linux:~/your-files/wordpress$ mysqldump --add-drop-table -h mysql-
hostserver -u mysql-username -p databasename > wp-database.sql
```

The above command will add the DROP TABLE option to the structure, will gather the required data from the database, and will dump the data into a file called wp-database.sql. Please be sure to add the correct name for your database server, username, and database name. It will prompt you for your password once you press *Enter*.

As before, hang on to that SQL file. We will need it momentarily.

Hosting and domain names

There is no shortage of web hosting companies and domain name registrars on the Internet. Many new hosts appear each day, and at the dawn of each day, some hosts disappear. Web hosting companies have practically become a "dime a dozen", but the advantage is that consumers have a broad choice when shopping for web hosting.

The basic types of web hosting one can buy exist in a hierarchy. Ranging from least-to-most expensive, the hierarchy is:

1. Shared hosting
2. Virtual private or Virtual dedicated server
3. Dedicated server

Shared hosting is exactly what it sounds like: the hosting space and resources that you purchase are "shared" with hundreds, or perhaps even thousands, of other customers per server. This may sound like a disaster waiting to happen, and it can be, but most of the time it works just fine provided that no single customer or website consumes too many resources at once. As the traffic needs of most websites are minimal, customers on shared servers can coexist peacefully.

If you are expecting hundreds of simultaneous customers on your site, or just distrust shared hosting in general, you should consider paying for a virtual private server. Though it's more costly, the benefit is that some of your resources (such as a certain amount of system RAM) are dedicated, and you can take comfort in knowing that you are only one of a dozen customers who are utilizing a given server.

If you are lucky enough to expect a booming business right from the start, then a server dedicated entirely to your sole usage may lie in your future. One can easily pay upwards of $100 each month for a dedicated server. However, if you are attracting enough customers to merit it, it's a worthwhile investment.

Most of us start, and even stay, with shared hosting. No matter which type of hosting you choose, be sure to consider the variety of criteria involved when choosing a web host, such as how much space and bandwidth they offer, their policies on resource consumption and CPU time, whether or not they require you to commit to a minimum contract term, any setup fees, and their responsiveness to support tickets.

A few popular web hosts include:

- DreamHost (`www.dreamhost.com`)
- Media Temple (`www.mediatemple.net`)
- A Small Orange (`www.asmallorange.com`)
- Lunarpages (`www.lunarpages.com`)

Keep in mind that you can often find coupons for discounts on hosting, so keep your eyes open.

In conjunction with web hosting, you will also need to own a domain name. If you do not have one already, it's time to head to a domain name registrar and see what's available. Competition is fierce concerning domain name prices, which typically hover around $9 to $10 per year. You can often get a slight discount for purchasing multiple years in advance.

A few popular domain name registrars include:

- GoDaddy (`www.godaddy.com`)
- Namecheap (`www.namecheap.com`)
- 1&1 Internet (`www.1and1.com`)

After purchasing a domain name, you must update your name servers at your registrar to point to your hosting package. Your web host should give you specific name server information, typically in the form of something like: `ns1.your-web-host.com`.

Uploading your shop

Now that we have web hosting and a domain name, it's time to officially transfer from the testing platform to the production server. This process will involve:

1. Setting up a new database

2. Importing your WordPress database

3. Uploading your WordPress files

4. Editing your `wp-config.php` file

Setting up a new database

With your web browser, log in to your web host's control panel. Your host may use cPanel, or Plesk, or a custom control panel. No matter the case, navigate to the database section. You may only see a MySQL logo, or maybe a link called **Manage Databases** as follows:

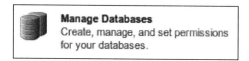

Within that section, you should be able to create a new empty database as well as a new database user:

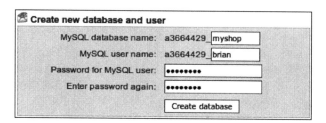

Some web hosts may automatically assign user privileges to the database. If your host requires that you manually assign user privileges, go ahead and do so now. The only database privileges required are **select**, **insert**, **delete**, **update**, **create**, **drop**, and **alter**, so try not to grant ALL privileges to that database user unless you do not have a choice. Once this process is finished, we will have an empty database in which to import our previous data.

Importing your WordPress database

It's time to upload and import our database. Remember, this file holds our posts, pages, products, and other settings, so it's critical that it imports properly!
If you have phpMyAdmin available on the production server, this process is a point-and-click affair.

Launch phpMyAdmin and select your newly created (and empty) database in the left-hand column. Now look near the top for the **Import** button:

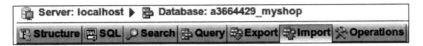

On the **Import** page, you should see a section titled **File to import**. Click on the **Browse** button and select the database file that we had exported earlier. The file type will be detected automatically, so there is no need to remove the SQL file from the archive, if applicable. An `*sql.gz` file is just fine:

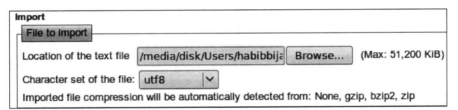

Click on **Go** at the bottom of the page to start the import process. Depending on the size of your database, it might take a few minutes to upload and process the data. When the process completes successfully, the content of the new database will be a replica of the old.

> Your web host may have limitations as to the size of the database file that you can upload. If your import fails because the file is too large, return to the export process and choose to export your database in chunks using only a few tables at a time. You can then import multiple smaller files, bypassing the problem and keeping your original database intact.

If you have shell access to your web hosting account, you can also import your WordPress database using the command line:

```
user@yourhost:~$ mysql -h mysql-hostserver -u mysql-username -p
databasename < wp-database.sql
```

Uploading your WordPress files

We're halfway finished with the process of getting our store online for the world to see. Right now our database is ready, but without the supporting WordPress files. Therefore, we ultimately have nothing but an empty website. In order to transfer the files to the new server, we need to use an FTP program. Two popular programs for transferring files are:

- FileZilla (`http://filezilla-project.org`) — available for Windows, Mac, and Linux

- Cyberduck (`http://cyberduck.ch`) — Mac only

Your web host should provide you with a username and password that you can use to connect via FTP. With this login information in hand, it's time to connect to your host and upload the files. Within FileZilla (or an FTP program of your choice), navigate to the root directory of your server (usually a `public_html` folder) and upload your files:

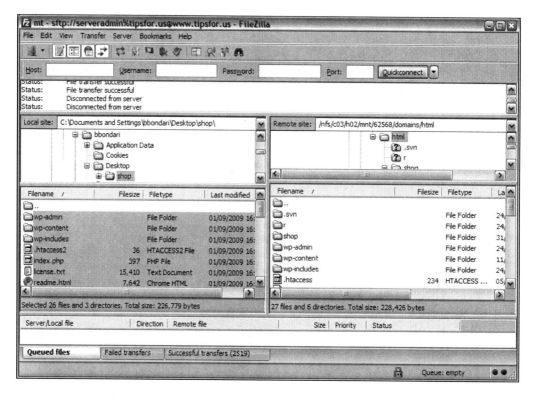

It may take several minutes for your files to upload, but once they finish, we only have one remaining task before the site goes live.

All web hosts should allow you to connect via FTP. If your host grants you shell (SSH) access, you can tell your FTP client to connect via sFTP, which adds an additional layer of security to all connections and file transfers. FTP-SLL is another secure option.

Editing your WordPress config file

Right now, your WordPress database has been imported and your files are in place, all that is left is to tell your uploaded WordPress files how to connect to the new database. We're so close, yet so far. To make this essential connection happen, we need to edit the file called `wp-config.php`. It is located within the root of your WordPress folder. This critical file contains information about your MySQL database, including your database username and password.

You can open this file with any text editor, such as Notepad++ (Windows), Smultron (Mac), or vanilla Notepad. Within your `wp-config.php` file, look for the MySQL settings and change them to your appropriate new database information:

```
// ** MySQL settings - You can get this info from your web host ** //
/** The name of the database for WordPress */
define('DB_NAME', 'your-db-name');

/** MySQL database username */
define('DB_USER', 'your-db-username');

/** MySQL database password */
define('DB_PASSWORD', 'your-db-password');

/** MySQL hostname */
define('DB_HOST', 'your-db-hostname');
```

Be sure to save the file once you have updated it. If you edited the file on your personal computer, be sure to upload it again and overwrite the previous file.

The `wp-config.php` is without a doubt one of the most important files related to your WordPress installation. Keep a backup of that file safe at all times.

Now try accessing your site using your domain name. If your settings are correct, your online store should come to life. Congratulations, your shop has been deployed!

Now is a good time to re-activate all of your plugins, including the WP e-Commerce plugin. Give your site a test drive to ensure that it looks and acts just like it did on the testing platform.

Man the hatches—essential site security

Releasing your site to the public is a cause for celebration, but it is also a cause for concern. Because your site is now visible to the public, you have an added level of responsibility for the security of your site. Security is a focus because we must protect more than just our website. We must also protect our customers and our entire business.

User passwords

One of the simplest and most effective methods for strengthening the security of your WordPress installation is to increase the complexity of your passwords. This is especially important for users with administrative privileges. Imagine a worst-case scenario in which an unscrupulous person somehow intercepts your admin password. This person could destroy your site in seconds, and could also potentially walk away with sensitive customer data.

Weak passwords are easily guessed or accessed via a "brute force" dictionary attack. This attack happens when an automated computer program rapidly guesses thousands of common words or phrases in an attempt to break into the system. What, then, differentiates a strong password from a weak one?

A strong password:

- Is at least 8-10 characters in length
- Uses a healthy mixture of letters (in both uppercase and lowercase) and numbers
- Uses some special characters (such as $, &, @, and #)
- Is unique (not recycled again and again for multiple sites)
- Does not contain words in any language, unless those words are misspelled or otherwise altered
- Does not contain any sensitive information (for instance, don't use your SSN as your password!)

One good suggestion is to consider using a password managing program to help you remember your password(s) if you have difficulty recalling them. Programs such as KeePass (`http://keepass.info`) can even generate massively strong passwords for you, far more complicated, and therefore harder to crack, than most people can typically remember.

The following is an example of the KeePass password generator in action:

Rename or replace the admin user

Here's another simple suggestion for increasing your site's security: rename or replace your admin account. If you set up WordPress manually, your default username is *admin*. Given that WordPress is an incredibly popular platform, how many "admin" accounts must exist out there? Thousands, if not tens or hundreds of thousands. This makes it a popular username for scripted cracking attempts. If your username is *admin*, the script is already half right, and all that lies in between your store and potential doom is the strength of your password. Scary thought, isn't it?

We can lessen, but not eliminate, this risk by renaming or replacing our admin account. If you wish to simply rename the admin account, you can do so in phpMyAdmin by finding the **user_login** field and changing the value from **admin** to whatever username you prefer:

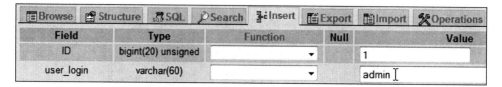

If you would rather not mess with phpMyAdmin, there's another easy way to change your default login: replace the admin user entirely. To do so, create a brand new user account with administrative privileges and give it a strong password. Now, log out of your account called *admin* and log in with your newly created account. Navigate to the **Users** section of WordPress and delete the old admin user.

Before WordPress actually deletes the account, it will prompt you to assign all existing content to a different user:

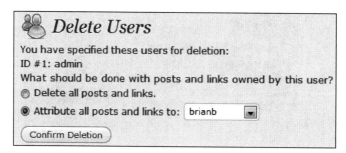

Make sure your newly created user is selected for content attribution, and then click on **Confirm Deletion**. Voila! Your "admin" account now has a different username, and that's one less thing to worry about with regard to security.

One related idea to make WordPress more secure is to maintain the old admin account, but to reduce its user role to that of Subscriber. That way, if someone manages to break into the account called admin, they are rendered useless. For more on users and roles, see Chapter 5, *User Accounts: Customers and Staff*.

WordPress and plugin updates

By far, the simplest and most inexcusable task that you can perform regularly to help keep your shop secure is to stay current with WordPress and third-party plugin updates. WordPress updates used to be a necessary inconvenience involving uploading the core files again to the server, but since the advent of WordPress version 2.7, core updates are essentially a one-click affair. Because of this added convenience, there are few reasons why one should not stay current. WordPress is developed with security in mind, but like all software, vulnerabilities are discovered over time and must be patched.

Whenever a new update is available, WordPress will notify you with a banner across the top of your Dashboard. In most cases, running an update only takes a click or two, and the entire process takes only a few seconds.

WordPress plugins are a similar story. Whenever a plugin update is ready, you will see a notification in red next to the **Plugins** section of your Dashboard informing you how many updates are available:

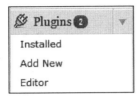

Unless you have reason to believe a plugin update will malfunction or conflict with some other aspect of your site, there's no reason not to keep your plugins current, either.

SSL for Dashboard login

Another excellent idea is to enable SSL for your domain. SSL stands for **Secure Sockets Layer**. It is a protocol for ensuring secure communication over the Internet. Most communications for regular browsing are not encrypted and can potentially be read by snooping third parties. When SSL becomes involved, the communication is encrypted and can only be decrypted and read by the server, thus greatly increasing security when dealing with sensitive information such as usernames and passwords.

As mentioned in Chapter 6, *Checkout and Payment Setup*, you will need a dedicated SSL certificate if you want to use certain payment gateways, such as **Chronopay** or **Authorize.net**. Dedicated SSL certificates are not free. You can expect to pay $30 to $50 per year for a certificate that is valid for a single domain. If you know that you own such a certificate, and you know that it has been set up properly (try accessing your domain using `https://`), you can force WordPress to use SSL when logging into the Dashboard by adding one single line to your `wp-config.php` file:

```
define('FORCE_SSL_ADMIN', true);
```

The "true" part of the parameter above will force your browser to switch to `https` when attempting to log into WordPress, thereby making it much more difficult for prying eyes to intercept your username and password.

Some web hosts offer a *shared* SSL option, which does not cost anything other than your regular monthly hosting fees. If you have a shared SSL certificate available (ask your host how to configure it), you could try the Admin SSL plugin for WordPress (`http://www.kerrins.co.uk/blog/admin-ssl`). This plugin works with both shared and dedicated SSL.

Eliminate directory browsing

One final security procedure we can quickly implement is to eliminate the possibility of someone browsing the contents of a directory on your server just by accessing the directory name. What's the potential problem? Let's say you have a folder called `mydata` on the server. If that folder does not have an `index.html` or `index.php` file within it, there's a possibility that a user who discovers the URL straight to that `mydata` folder could view the contents of all the individual files within that folder.

Specific to WordPress, this used to be a problem in that someone could browse straight to your `plugins` folder and immediately view all of the plugins running on your site. Newer versions of WordPress have fixed this problem by adding empty `index.php` files to most folders, but this could still be a problem with any non-WordPress sections of your site.

Some web hosts automatically restrict browsing of directories. To find out whether or not your host allows it, simply create a new folder somewhere in the root directory of your site. Add a few *non-index* files to it and then type in the URL that would lead you to that particular folder. If you get an error message, that's a good sign. If you can see the names of the files that you added to that folder, then it's time to implement a simple security measure.

Find a file in your root directory (for example, the `public_html` folder) called
`.htaccess`. Depending on your FTP program, you may need to enable the viewing
of hidden files to see the `.htaccess` file. Open it with any text editor and add this
single line to it:

```
Options All -Indexes
```

This single line of code affects all folders and sub-folders in your web hosting
account, restricting the behavior to not allow anyone to browse directories and view
their contents. It will not affect the typical functionality of your site in any capacity.

Backups—preparing for disasters

Despite all of our security measures, there is still one important piece missing: data
backup. All of the security measures in the world cannot protect us from data loss.
After all, computer parts eventually and often unexpectedly fail. Surely we have all
experienced that unpleasant surprise on some level in our lives.

Yes, data loss can (and does) happen on a daily basis. It is inevitable. However, we
can prepare for it and should not relegate data backup as the sole responsibility of
our web hosting provider. Most good web hosts do regularly back up their servers,
but they are not immune to catastrophic hardware failures. No, backups are our
responsibility. Imagine how much better you will sleep at night knowing that your
entire business is not at risk of literally disappearing overnight!

There are two major components of data backup involving WordPress: the database
and the regular files on the server.

Database backup and restoration

If you have completed this chapter up to this point, then you already have a backup
of your database, and exported it either via phpMyAdmin or via the command line.
All you need to do is follow those same steps that we completed earlier to create
another database backup.

But wouldn't it be nice if we could automate this process so that we don't need to
remember to manually back up everything? We can.

One method is to use the excellent WP-DB-Backup plugin (`http://www.ilfilosofo.com/blog/wp-db-backup`). This plugin not only allows you to manually back up the database from within the WordPress Dashboard, but it allows you to create scheduled automatic backups, e-mailed straight to you:

Scheduled Backup

Schedule:
- ○ Never
- ○ Once Hourly
- ○ Twice Daily
- ● Once Daily
- ○ Once Weekly

Email backup to: your@email.com

(Schedule backup)

Tables to include in the scheduled backup:
Click and hold down [SHIFT] to toggle multiple checkboxes

- ☑ wp_MailPress_mailmeta
- ☑ wp_MailPress_mails
- ☑ wp_MailPress_stats
- ☑ wp_MailPress_usermeta
- ☑ wp_MailPress_users
- ☑ wp_newsUsers
- ☑ wp_newscategories
- ☑ wp_nl_email

Just choose a **Schedule**, select the database **Tables to include in the scheduled backup**, enter your e-mail address, and click on the **Schedule backup** button. The plugin will take care of everything else and will send the backup to your provided e-mail account. You can restore that database at any time using phpMyAdmin or via the command line.

That takes care of the database, but we still need to find ways to back up our regular site files.

Server data backup and restoration

With the database out of the way, let's discuss some possible options for regularly creating copies of our files and folders on the server. Most web hosts provide a way in their control panel to archive and download all your site files in one fell swoop. If your host uses the popular **cPanel** option, look for the **Backups** icon:

Backups

With cPanel at your disposal, you can easily download an entire home directory anytime you desire. cPanel also has an elegant way to restore an existing home directory backup. The naming conventions vary, but you might see an option for "Home Directory Restore" or **1-Click Website Restore**:

All you need to do is **Browse** to select a previously downloaded backup file (as seen below) and upload it. cPanel will restore it, overwriting existing files in your home directory.

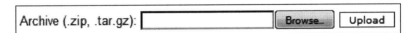

 cPanel also offers one-click downloads and restores of MySQL databases.

A second option is to use your FTP program of choice to download backups of your site on demand. Just connect to your web host, select the folders that you wish to transfer, and choose where to save them on your local machine.

Yet another option is to use a program such as WinSCP (http://winscp.net) to create a sync point between your website and your local machine. This creates a backup "mirror" of your site files, ensuring that you always have the latest copy of your site in a convenient location.

Which backup method should you use? Pick one, or maybe use all of them! In fact, you should keep multiple backups available at any given time. In a perfect world, we wouldn't need to worry about file backups, but if disaster strikes, you don't want to be without one.

Summary

We covered a lot of ground in this chapter, and it's a huge accomplishment to get your store up and running! We successfully migrated and transferred both the WordPress database and all of the site files from the testing platform to the production server. Once our site went live, we also performed some necessary adjustments to bolster our site's security. We then found several ways to protect our data even more by creating multiple backups of all essential files. In case disaster occurs, we won't lose anything critical and can quickly restore our business without starting over from scratch.

This chapter covered:

- Getting ready to deploy—including last-minute WordPress tweaks, exporting your database, and thoughts on web hosting
- Uploading your shop—details on creating and importing your database, uploading your files, and getting your new site running
- Man the hatches—a few necessary adjustments to decrease the chances of someone breaking into your site
- Backups—some vital information on how to prepare for and recover from catastrophic data loss

At this point, you should feel good because your shop is now ready to cater to customers and generate business.

Up next we'll tip our hats to some of WP e-Commerce's competition by exploring some alternative e-Commerce plugins.

10
Alternative e-Commerce Plugins

The WP e-Commerce plugin is an impressive and ambitious piece of software. However, as with any ambitious software project, bugs will occasionally rear their ugly heads and certain releases will undoubtedly be better than others. Without a doubt, the developers at Instinct should be commended for their hard work in creating the WP e-Commerce plugin, and especially for releasing a version that is completely free.

That said, your humble author believes that we all benefit from choice and competition, and there's more than one e-commerce plugin in town that can integrate with WordPress. While we believe strongly in the long-term viability of the WP e-Commerce plugin, we think it is right to let budding shop owners know about competing software products.

There are several competing software programs worth mentioning. The majority of them are free (or at least offer a free version in addition to a paid upgrade), but a couple of them cost money. All of them are worth your time and effort to investigate.

This chapter covers the following software programs:

- YAK (Yet Another Kart)
- eShop
- Shopp
- WordPress Simple PayPal Shopping Cart
- Market Theme

For each alternative plugin, we will provide a feature highlight and discuss how these features compare to WP e-Commerce. In a few cases, we will also cover basic setup and usage.

YAK (Yet Another Kart)

More information: `http://bit.ly/wp-yak`

Like WP e-Commerce, **YAK (Yet Another Kart)** is a full-featured plugin for WordPress. Unlike WP e-Commerce, YAK is completely opensource and does not have any paid upgrades. Certain features lacking in the free version of WP e-Commerce, such as Product Search, come by default in YAK.

The plugin is mainly the work of a single developer, and although YAK is completely free, the developer offers a detailed handbook for sale on his site (`http://bit.ly/yak-handbook`).

What YAK offers

The YAK plugin offers features comparable to, though fewer than, those of WP e-Commerce. Philosophically, the main difference between YAK and WP e-Commerce is that YAK associates all products with posts or pages within WordPress. Instead of creating products directly in the WordPress Dashboard, you just write a new post or page with the product details, adding the price and "buy now" button using text tags. One benefit of this method is that customers can use the standard WordPress search box to easily search for products.

A few other highlights of YAK include the ability to automatically sell product downloads (such as MP3 files); the ability to create coupons to provide discounts on product price or shipping; and slick, Flash-based charts displaying your sales reports. Speaking of sales, YAK integrates with PayPal Standard, PayPal Pro, Authorize.net, and (basic) Google Checkout.

Basic YAK setup and usage

Getting started with YAK is pretty simple. First, install it like any other plugin for WordPress, either by uploading it manually or by using the built-in plugin installer. Once it's installed, you will see new entries for **Yak General** and **Yak Shipping** under **Settings** in your WordPress Dashboard.

Just as with WP e-Commerce, there are a few initial settings that you should configure. First of all, switch to the **Basic** tab at the top to configure the **Basic Settings**:

Most of the settings displayed on this page are self-explanatory. At the least, you should be sure to add a confirmation e-mail and order confirmation message, choose a default product category name, and select an option for the handling of order numbers.

The settings for **Products price/quantity** are especially important, as they control your currency details. One common pitfall deals with the **Auto discount** option, which you can use to automatically offer discounts on your entire product catalog. In a new install of YAK, the **Auto discount** is set to **0.9**, thereby granting a slight discount on all of your products. If none of the products on your site display the actual price that you set, this is likely the culprit. Set the **Auto discount** option to **1** to disable automatic discounts.

The rest of the page deals with currency settings, which you can alter to fit your needs, as shown in the following screenshot:

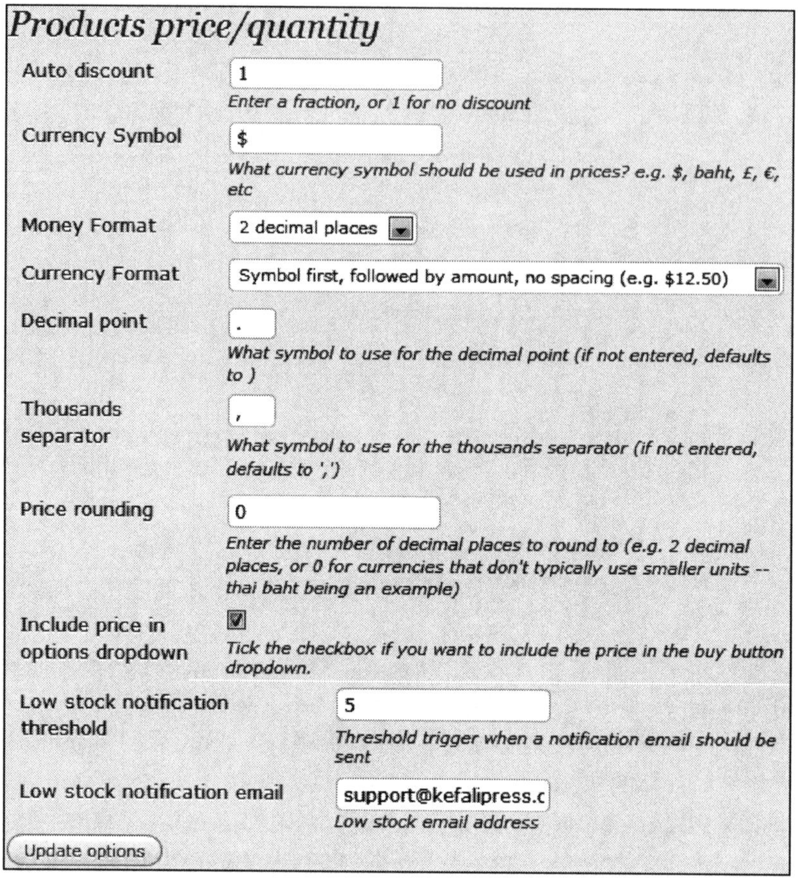

Adding a new product with YAK

As mentioned earlier, the underlying philosophical difference between YAK and WP e-Commerce is that YAK associates products with individual posts or pages. Therefore, adding a new item to sell only entails adding a new post!

In your WordPress Dashboard, create a new post, giving it a descriptive title for your product. In the body of the post, add any pertinent details about the item. You can use the standard WordPress image uploader to add any number of pictures. In order to make the post e-Commerce friendly, you need to add two short tags within the post body. The first one is **[yak_price]**, which displays the price for the item, and the other is **[yak_buy]**, which displays an *Add to cart* button:

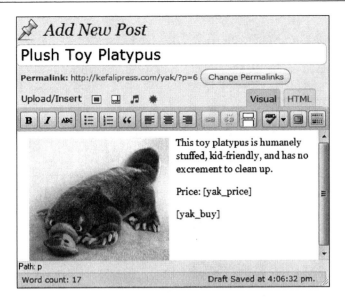

Before you publish the post, the final task is to scroll down to the **YAK Product Details** section below the post. Here you can set the price for the item, as well as add a product weight and set an inventory number:

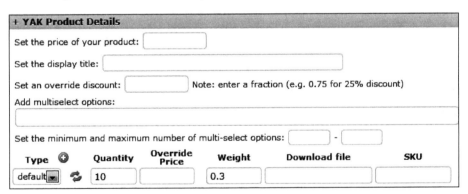

If you wish, you can also set an alternate display title. Provided that your product is a digital download, you can set the absolute path to the file on your server under the **Download file** section.

The absolute path to the digital download is how you might locate the file on your web server. Ideally, this file is not directly accessible via the Web, as you do not want anyone discovering the path to your file(s) without paying first. If you are not sure how to discover the absolute path, ask your web host.

Once you publish the post, your new item is available for customers to purchase. Here's how an example looks on our site:

This concludes our brief section on YAK. Though its features are outnumbered by WP e-Commerce, it's still a capable and impressive plugin.

eShop

More information: `http://bit.ly/e-shop`

Like YAK, eShop is another completely open-source plugin for WordPress. There are no paid upgrades available that increase functionality, though some sites sell WordPress themes designed specifically for eShop.

eShop is mainly the product of a single developer and is marketed as a plugin created with ease of use and accessibility in mind.

What eShop offers

eShop shares YAK's general philosophy of associating individual products with WordPress posts. Once again, the advantage of this method is that your products are easily *searchable* using the built-in WordPress search box.

Other general features of eShop include support for digital downloads, configurable e-mail templates, automatic e-mail delivery after item purchase, support for coupons and discounts, and integration with Google Base. There are several payment gateways that eShop supports, but the most mainstream amongst them are PayPal and Authorize.net. On the other hand, eShop supports a few esoteric gateways that other plugins do not, such as Payson and eProcessingNetwork.

Basic eShop setup and usage

Getting started with eShop is as easy as, if not easier than, YAK. The first step is to install the eShop plugin just like you would any other plugin for WordPress. Once it's installed, you will see in your Dashboard an **eShop** link under **Settings** and a full, expandable **eShop** side menu, as shown in the following screenshot:

There are only a few minor settings to configure before you can hit the ground running. To get started, click on the **eShop** link under **Settings** to make a few basic configuration changes.

On the **eShop Settings** page, you will notice eShop's status is set to **Testing**, and the default payment gateway is PayPal.

Keep the status in mind, since you will eventually want to switch from **Testing** mode to **Live** before you start earning income.

A few essential settings that you should consider on this page are an e-mail address for the messages sent automatically from the shop, an appropriate currency symbol, and any elements dealing with stock control.

On the **Merchant Gateways** page, be sure to set your country, your desired currency, and your preferred payment gateway.

Those are the minimal settings you need to configure. Now you can start adding products.

Adding a new product with eShop

Just as with YAK, adding a new product to your eShop store begins by creating a new post in WordPress. Unlike YAK, we do not need to worry about adding text tags to the body of the post. Just give the post a descriptive title and add as much content as you want to the post body. Pictures can all be uploaded using the standard WordPress image uploader.

Attaching the actual product information to the post is handled by the **Product Entry** settings below the post body. Here, you can add a unique identifier for your item (**Sku**) as well as a description that will be sent to your payment processor. You can also add a few options to your item with a variation of prices.

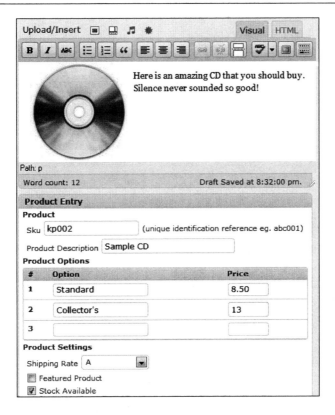

Before you publish the post and release your product to the world, be sure to select the **Stock Available** checkbox. Otherwise, eShop will think you are out of stock.

With the item published, here is how it looks on a site:

This brings our section on eShop to a close. As with YAK, it falls a few features short of WP e-Commerce, but we commend the developers for their hard work. eShop is truly an impressive plugin.

Shopp

More information: `http://shopplugin.net`

Shopp is one of only two e-Commerce options mentioned here that is commercial-only and unavailable in a free version. The current price for a single-site license is $55, whereas a developer's license is $299.

The plugin also has a multitude of additional payment gateways and shipping modules available for $25 per add-on. Shopp is undoubtedly nice, but is also potentially very expensive.

What Shopp offers

Even without the optional add-ons, Shopp offers a plethora of features. Shopp shares WP e-Commerce's core philosophy of building the product catalog in the WordPress Dashboard, though you can also use shortcodes to add specific products to individual posts or pages. Like every plugin mentioned so far, Shopp supports both physical products and digital downloads. The shopping cart is also AJAX-enabled, meaning that it features drag-and-drop shopping. Keep in mind that WP e-Commerce also offers AJAX support with their optional DropShop 2.0 module.

Shopp also offers the standard features that one would expect a commercial-only offering to provide, such as automatic e-mail notifications, product search, lots of template tags, order history, and tons of Dashboard and theme widgets.

Payment gateways that come with Shopp by default include: PayPal Standard and Express, Google Checkout, and 2Checkout. Many other gateways are available as paid add-ons, including Authorize.net, PayPal Pro, HSBC ePayments, and PayJunction.

Shopp certainly has a lot to offer. Feature-wise, it compares favorably with WP e-Commerce, though the lack of a free offering will undoubtedly turn some customers away.

WordPress Simple PayPal Shopping Cart

More information: `http://bit.ly/wpspsc`

Despite the deceptively long name, **WordPress Simple PayPal Shopping Cart (WPSPSC)** is exactly what it claims to be: a simple shopping cart integration for WordPress that allows customers to purchase items using PayPal. It actually takes longer to describe how to use it than it takes to learn and master it. This plugin is free.

For the record, WPSPSC does have a bigger brother called WP e-Store (`http://bit.ly/e-store`) that allows for the sale of both physical goods and digital downloads. The current price is a very reasonable $29.95.

What WordPress Simple PayPal Shopping Cart offers

Don't expect a long feature list here—the key word is simplicity. WPSPSC follows the philosophy of "do one thing and do it well". It does not provide support for the sale of digital downloads. It does not generate order reports, automatically e-mail customers after a sale (it relies on PayPal to do that), or even provide an inventory catalog.

What this program does is provide an easy way to slap a shopping cart onto WordPress and start selling products. Its minimal features can be seen as an advantage—there are fewer bugs that can be introduced, and learning how to use the plugin takes mere seconds.

Basic WordPress Simple PayPal Shopping Cart setup and usage

You know the drill by now—install WPSPSC just like any other WordPress plugin. Once it's installed, you should see a new entry for **WP Shopping Cart** under **Settings** in your Dashboard, as seen below.

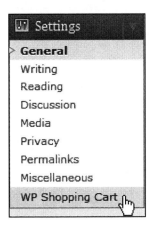

That link will lead you to a shocking *single-page* of configuration settings. You will likely only have to alter one or two settings, particularly your currency settings or your PayPal e-mail address, as seen in the following screenshot:

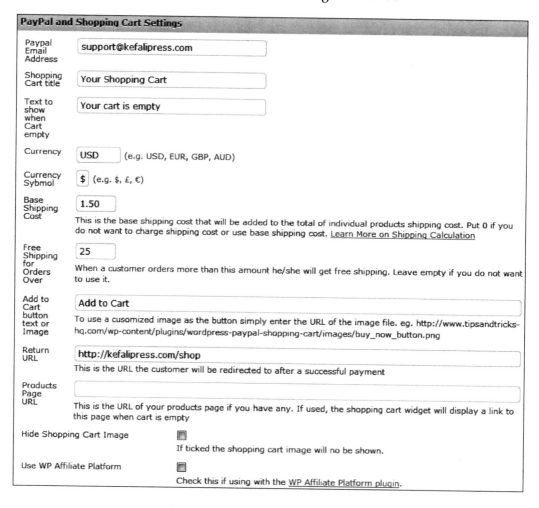

Next, you need to choose a location for your actual shopping cart. If you want it to reside in a sidebar widget, the plugin includes one just for that purpose. You can also dedicate a separate post or page for it—just create a new "Shopping Cart" post or page and add this tag to it: `[show_wp_shopping_cart]`

The shopping cart will appear wherever that tag or widget is used.

Adding a new product with WPSPSC

Listing a new product with WPSPSC resembles YAK and eShop in that you add the product information to individual posts in WordPress. However, as mentioned earlier, WPSPSC does not have a centralized product catalog. Instead, it relies on another text tag to interpret the product name and price.

Begin by adding a new post to WordPress. After you have chosen an appropriate title and body description for your product, it's time to add the text tag. Here's how it works:

```
[wp_cart:PRODUCT-NAME:price:PRODUCT-PRICE:end]
```

That bit of text is how WPSPSC interprets the name and price of your item. You only need to replace PRODUCT-NAME with the actual name and PRODUCT-PRICE with a numerical price.

 This tag will only look like an "Add to Cart" button to the customer, so it's strongly recommended to type the actual product name and price into the body of the post as well, so as to not confuse the customer.

Let's put it into action; here is a new post with the product name and price included:

Once we publish the post, the tag turns into an **Add to Cart** button. If you add that item to the shopping cart, it appears inside your widget, ready to proceed to PayPal:

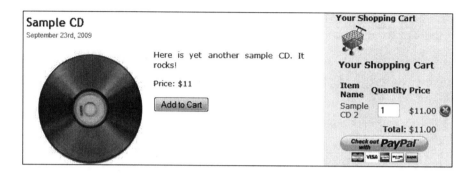

That covers 99 percent of the typical usage for WPSPSC. It gets only slightly more complicated if you want to add variations to your items, such as size or color.

Overall, WordPress Simple PayPal Shopping Cart lives up to its name and works very well. The lack of a centralized product catalog is both a strength and a weakness—a strength because it has fewer moving parts to break, and a weakness because a shop owner with lots of items will likely find it unwieldy. However, someone with only a few items to sell could easy fall in love with this plugin.

Market Theme

More information: http://www.markettheme.com

This last plugin is not actually a plugin at all, but really just a theme for WordPress. First released in early 2008, the Market Theme harnesses the power of WordPress' custom fields to great effect. The result is the complete integration of an e-Commerce platform into WordPress, without the need to install a single plugin. They do offer a complementary plugin to help manage products, but it is not required.

No doubt this is an impressive feat, and they charge for it. The Market Theme is the second software package mentioned in this chapter that is commercial-only. There are two license types available: Standard and Developer. A Standard license is currently $55 and allows a single person to build one or more stores across multiple domains, provided they are all in use by that same individual. The Developer license (currently $150) allows for reselling, as is typical when someone builds a store for a client.

What the Market Theme offers

Though it's just a theme, Market is not light on features. It offers support for both physical and digital products, product search by default, support for product variations, and a grid-based layout for your products (available in WP e-Commerce with the Gold Cart upgrade). It also comes with an AJAX shopping cart module.

Concerning payment gateways, Market currently only interfaces with PayPal Standard and Google Checkout, though they have plans to add more gateways in the future. Once you purchase a license, the developers of the Market Theme will grant you free lifetime upgrades, so there's never a need to worry about repurchasing the product to gain access to newly developed features.

Because Market is a theme for WordPress, you are able to edit and modify it to your heart's content. Though they do not offer a free version, they do have an online demo (available at: `http://www.markettheme.com/demo`) that you can try before you buy.

Summary

As you can see, WP e-Commerce has plenty of competitors, but it is competition that drives these products to become better. Though we are fond of WP e-Commerce, we welcome these competitors and congratulate them on their success. We all benefit as a result.

Chapter 10 covered:

- YAK (Yet Another Kart)—an odd name for an e-Commerce plugin, but an impressive product, for free.
- eShop—another open-source plugin. Very user-friendly and for free.
- Shopp—powerful and elegant, yet commercial-only.
- WordPress Simple PayPal Shopping Cart—simplicity epitomized. It's short on features, and it's supposed to be that way.
- Market Theme—a theme to the extreme, and not an actual plugin. It is commercial only.

No matter which plugin you use to power your new online store, we still have one major issue left to consider: how to bring customers through our virtual doors. In Chapter 11, we will cover marketing your new shop.

11
Marketing Your Shop

As satisfying as it is to get your online store running, the work is not yet complete. Up to this point, you've labored and toiled in building your shop, wrestling with configuration settings, plus deploying and securing your shop. You should definitely congratulate yourself on all of the time and effort you have invested thus far. However, as anyone who has built a successful online store already knows, the initial effort invested up to the store deployment date is only the beginning of a journey that will hopefully pay rich dividends for the rest of your entrepreneurial life.

With apologies to the popular movie from 1989 *Field of Dreams*, the mantra "if you build it, [they] will come" does not automatically hold true for new store owners. We would all be gleefully happy if it were. Let's face it, most new stores receive little to no traffic at first. It's a rare store indeed that already has a solidly established customer base upon first launch. What steps, then, can we take in order to start attracting new customers?

The first step is to simply take a deep breath and accept the fact that our stores are almost guaranteed not to start generating hundreds of sales overnight. Once we get past that mental hurdle, we free ourselves from feelings of initial dissatisfaction and frustration. That's right, it's *normal* not to see dozens of active users on your website statistic tracker at any given time immediately after launch. It's *normal* not to make your first sale for days, or even weeks after launch. This does *not* mean that your store is a failure and that you should move on to other ventures.

That said, all of us want to start attracting customers to our sites and to start making sales. So what can we do to get that process rolling? Many people have dedicated their lives to the study of marketing and advertising, and while you don't need to be an expert marketer, there are a number of easy steps that you can take to help new potential customers find your store or become repeat customers. Some of them inevitably cost money, but many of them are completely free and are already integrated within the WP e-Commerce plugin.

This chapter covers:

- Coupons and discounts
- Cross sales
- Built-in 'Share This' plugin
- Purchasing advertising
- Email, newsletters, and blogging

Coupons and discounts

One of the simplest and most effective ways to attract a customer's attention is to offer coupon codes for discounts on your products. Likely, we have all seen these in action before at our favorite online retailers. The basic premise is that the customer can enter a valid code during the checkout process to get a discount on a single item or on the entire order. The code that you create could be valid for only one use or for a set period of time.

To create a coupon for customer usage, first log into your WordPress Dashboard and browse to the **Marketing** link under the **Products** menu, as shown in the following screenshot:

Next, click the **Add Coupon** link, as shown in the following screenshot:

Let's say that we want to create a coupon that grants a **10%** discount for the entire order during the month of August. We'll call the coupon **AUGUST10**.

To add a coupon with these parameters to our store we must follow these steps. First, enter the text for the coupon title under the **Coupon Code** section. Next, enter a value for the discount and choose from the drop-down list whether you want it to be in cash value or as a percentage discount, as shown in the following screenshot:

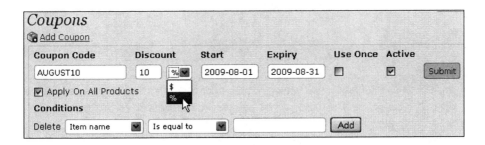

The **Start** and **Expiry** dates for the coupon are potentially the most confusing. Ideally, this should be a point and click affair for choosing dates, but perhaps a future plugin update will address this. As of now, enter the beginning and ending dates in the following numerical format: YEAR-MONTH-DAY. For example, if our desired starting date is August 1, 2009, then we would enter it as: **2009-08-01**. Make sense?

If you want the coupon to be valid for one usage only, be sure to select the checkbox under **Use Once**. Otherwise, leave it blank. If you want the coupon to provide a discount for the entire order, be sure to select the checkbox next to **Apply On All Products**. When finished, be sure to click the **Submit** button.

 Keep in mind that all discounts for coupons are subtracted from the original product price (the subtotal), not including any additional costs for taxes and shipping.

When customers go through the checkout process, they will now have a place to enter an optional coupon code as shown in the following screenshot. This field will only be displayed if at least one coupon is currently active:

Simple as it is to offer a site-wide discount on all products, the WP e-Commerce plugin does offer a lot of fine-tuning with regard to coupons. Want to create a discount for only a specific item? Okay, how about offering a discount for customers who purchase more than four items at once? No problem.

Using conditions, you can customize your coupons to handle any number of possibilities. **Conditions** appear at the bottom of the coupon section and include three components: a factor, a variable, and a value.

The available factors are:

- Item name
- Item quantity
- Total quantity
- Subtotal amount

The available variables that can be attached to a factor are:

- Is equal to
- Is greater than
- Is less than
- Contains
- Does not contain
- Begins with
- Ends with

The value field is blank by default and it's up to you to set a value. When setting up such a customized coupon, your job is to pair one of the above factors with a variable and its relationship to the value that you provide. Sound complicated? It really isn't. Let's make this simpler with an illustration.

For instance, let's say that we want to create a coupon called **TAKEFIVE** that offers a **5%** discount, provided that the customer purchases at least five total items at once. The way we satisfy the full condition is as follows:

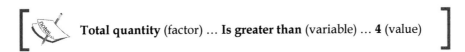

Total quantity (factor) ... **Is greater than** (variable) ... **4** (value)

When our **TAKEFIVE** coupon is active, a customer adding at least a total of five items to his cart can use this coupon to receive a slight discount. The **Conditions** options are shown in the following screenshot:

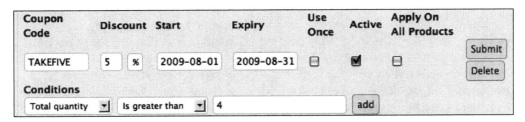

Here's another example. Let's say we want to create a $1 discount for anyone purchasing our *Ave Maria* sheet music. We will give the coupon the title of GRATIAPLENA and will set the following condition:

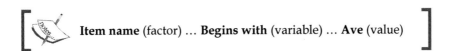

Item name (factor) ... **Begins with** (variable) ... **Ave** (value)

Make sense? The above condition could be troublesome if our sheet music store had multiple titles beginning with *Ave*, but as of now, it works. Another option could be to use the **Contains** variable and provide the full title.

As you can see, there are a number of ways to take advantage of coupons to provide discounts to your customers. In general, consumers love to get good deals. Therefore, don't discount the effectiveness of coupons in attracting traffic to your store. They're one of the simplest methods you have to draw shopper interest and create sales, even if it means taking a temporary loss on an item. Coupons can be part of an e-mail newsletter to existing customers, you can post them on your business blog, and you can submit them to popular online deal sites such as FatWallet (`http://www.fatwallet.com`) and SlickDeals (`http://slickdeals.net`) to help get the coupon out into the wild. If your deal is a good one, word will spread and you will receive a flood of interested traffic.

Keep in mind that you can further entice customers by creating an option to grant free shipping when the total order price meets or exceeds a certain amount. See Chapter 7, *Shipping, Taxes, and Collecting Payments* for details.

Cross sales

Enabling cross sales for your store is another simple option at your disposal for helping to increase sales. What are cross sales? Imagine that you are shopping at a popular online merchant such as *Amazon.com*. Whenever you view an individual item, further down the page you will find a list of other items that customers have purchased along with the current item. These are cross sales. The suggestion is to buy other items along with the current one.

Enabling cross sales is a one-click affair. Browse to the Marketing page, look under **Marketing Settings**, and switch the radio button for **Display Cross Sales** to **Yes** as shown in the following screenshot:

That's it. Unlike coupons, there are no other options or configuration settings. Once enabled, cross sales will begin displaying other items of potential interest to customers.

 The items displayed as part of cross sales are based on your existing sales history. It may take a little while for a brand new store to start displaying cross sales since there is little or no sales history. At this time there is no way to manually choose which products to display.

'Share This' plugin

Here is another quick and easy setting that you can enable to potentially drive new traffic to your store. The *Share This* plugin is popular amongst writers of general WordPress blog posts. It enables readers to save a post they like to numerous popular social bookmarking/networking sites like Delicious, StumbleUpon, Digg, and Facebook.

When enabled, the *Share This* plugin allows your customers to help spread the word about your products for you. To enable it, just set the option for **Show Share This (Social Bookmarks)** to **Yes,** as shown in the following screenshot:

On each individual product page, you will then see a **Share This Product** button just below the item price. Clicking the button expands the available sharing options. The following screenshot shows the **Share This Product** button:

Switching to the **E-mail** tab allows you (or a customer) to e-mail a direct link to that product to a friend.

Purchasing advertising

Up to this point, every technique that we have mentioned has been completely free. While it may be true that "the best things in life are free" (such as WordPress), it is an unfortunate fact that, at some point, you must spend money to make money. It's likely that you have already done so. For example, you own a domain name and pay for web hosting, don't you?

Yes, spending money to run an online store is necessary, but it's a small price to pay if the money you spend results in increased traffic and sales. Note that there is a world of difference between these two: traffic and sales. Some marketers push the idea of paying a company a set monetary value to drive traffic to their site. Many thousands of visitors a day are ultimately worthless if none of them purchase anything. Therein lies the problem with "purchased" traffic—who is to know whether those visitors have the slightest care or interest at all in your products? It's *quality* traffic that we are seeking, not necessarily quantity.

How, then, do we get quality traffic? Part of it is gained organically through such tried-and-true techniques such as word of mouth, coupons, e-mail campaigns, and running a business blog. Other quality traffic is earned through targeted Internet advertising. Two of the most popular targeted Internet advertising centers are Google AdWords and Microsoft adCenter. Let's discuss them now.

Google AdWords

The Google AdWords network (`http://adwords.google.com`) is one of the biggest and best advertising networks on the Internet. It's also very easy to set up and monitor a keyword campaign with them. Before you register, remember that you do need to pay for these ads, but the control of the cost is in your hands. There is a one-time $5 activation fee to start using AdWords, but there are no mandatory fees or minimum budgets beyond that. You only pay your agreed price per click, and you can disable ads at any time.

As you guessed, Google AdWords displays your ads on the Google search engine results page, within Gmail, and within other Google related services. The Google name is undoubtedly one of the most recognized brands in computing, so creating an AdWords campaign is destined to give your site some exposure. If you register with only one ad network, Google AdWords should be it.

Creating an AdWords account is totally free. It's only when you want your ad(s) to go live that Google charges the activation fee plus any cost-per-click fees. This means you are free to register for an account and familiarize yourself with AdWords by creating one or more campaigns without worrying about cost.

The ad setup process is easy. As part of the process, you are given an opportunity to customize your location and language preferences. If your store sells and ships products worldwide, you can advertise worldwide. On the other hand, if your store is designed to sell products mostly in one town or state/region, you can display ads only in that area. You can also set a daily budget and a specific date range in which Google should display your ads.

The crux of the setup process is in choosing how your ad should look. The following screenshot shows the options under the **Ads** tab:

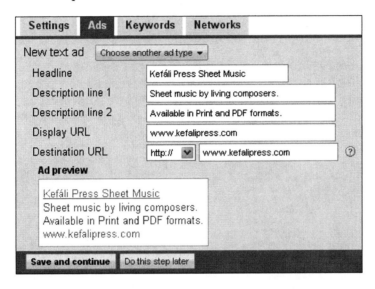

It's deceivingly difficult to write a good Google ad. Naturally, you want the customer to glean as much information about your store as possible, but you are limited to 70 characters per line. Keep in mind as well that your ad will likely be surrounded by ads from competitors, so you need to try to catch the customer's attention and prove that your store is better than the other choices , which is a formidable task in 70 characters or less.

One suggestion is to try to write a single Google ad in under 30 seconds. Chances are high that your first intuition on how to summarize your store in a sentence or two is best, and any time spent stewing over the "perfect" ad is wasted time. Plus, you can always write a new ad or revise the old one at a later date.

Microsoft adCenter

Similar to Google AdWords, Microsoft adCenter (`https://adcenter.microsoft.com/`) is a competing advertising network. The obvious difference between the AdWords and adCenter networks is that AdWords uses Google whereas adCenter uses Microsoft's Bing search engine and related services. Otherwise, you will find striking similarities between the two, including the initial $5 activation fee to start displaying ads.

Just as with AdWords, you can specify a region in which to advertise, choosing from the entire world, a specific state, or anywhere in between. You also have full control over your monthly budget and maximum price you wish to pay per ad click.

Registration is not required to start walking through the campaign setup process. You will only need to create an account once you have created and customized your first ad. Speaking of which, this process is also similar to AdWords, including the 70 character limit for the **Ad text**. The fields that need to be filled for creating an ad using adCenter are shown in the following screenshot:

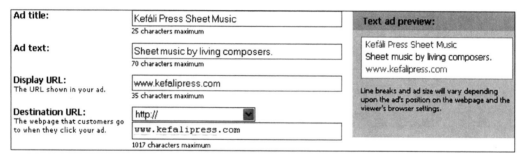

As with AdWords, you can also specify a number of keywords to associate with your ad. Microsoft adCenter also includes a host of tools to analyze and track the performance of your ad campaign.

Both AdWords and adCenter are popular tools for managing your Internet ads. By no means are they mutually exclusive, either. There's nothing stopping you from running ads on both networks. In fact, that's a *good* idea because it gives your store exposure on two of the most popular search engines. If you have not yet signed up for either network, keep your eyes peeled for coupons (see how effective they are?) granting you an initial monetary bonus. For instance, many web hosts now include complementary $50 to $100 advertising network vouchers just for purchasing web hosting. If you find a coupon, there's absolutely no reason not to take advantage of it.

E-mail, newsletters, and blogging

Another option to consider is to create and maintain an email newsletter to send to your subscribers. Having a newsletter is a fantastic way to let your visitors know about new coupon codes, special sales, new products, or any other worthy notifications. We're not talking about the scourge of the Internet that we all know and hate: SPAM. We are talking about an opt-in/opt-out system in which we can send store and product news to those readers who want them.

E-mail/newsletters

Creating an email newsletter campaign should not take up so much of your time that your store suffers. It can be as simple or as complicated as you need it to be. You can choose to handle everything yourself, or you can pay a third-party company to handle many of the tasks for you. Here are a few options:

1. Spreadsheet only
2. Find a plugin for WordPress
3. A third-party service

Let's take a look at these in detail:

Option 1: Spreadsheet only

This first option is the easiest to get started, though likely not the simplest to maintain. The only tools you need are a spreadsheet and a tiny form to collect subscriptions. Many WordPress plugins, such as Contact Form 7 (http://bit.ly/contact-form-7), allow you to create a form which will e-mail the results to you when a user completes it. With such a form, you can customize it to only contain the user's e-mail address and an option to either subscribe or unsubscribe to a newsletter.

Whenever you receive a notification, just copy the user's e-mail address to a spreadsheet. If you receive an "unsubscribe" notification, just delete that address in your spreadsheet. This method may be crude, but is very effective for smaller campaigns and is totally free. As your campaign numbers increase, you may want to look for a different solution.

A slick variation on this option is to embed a form from Google Docs (http://docs.google.com), which is completely free and only requires a Google account. The benefit of using Google Docs is that it will auto-populate your spreadsheet with the email addresses for you. All you need to do is copy and paste the column of addresses to your email client.

Create a new form, give it a title, and set only two "questions": one for the e-mail address and one for a "Yes or No" option, as shown in the following screenshot:

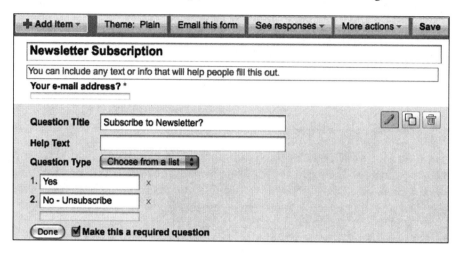

Once you have completed the form, find the code to embed it within WordPress. One way to find this code is by navigating to the **More actions** menu and choosing **Embed,** as shown in the following screenshot:

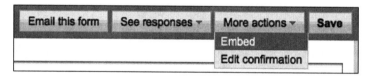

Copy the resulting code to your desired placement location within WordPress, such as a page or even its own text widget. The following screenshot shows how it will look on the front page of a site, in a sidebar widget:

As mentioned earlier, when visitors add their email addresses to this form, Google Docs will automatically dump it into a spreadsheet for you. Nice! The only caveat here is that Google Docs does not automatically remove an email address if the customer chooses the **Unsubscribe** option. It's up to you to manually delete it. Still, unless you are fortunate enough to have thousands of subscribers, it's an easy problem to manage.

Option 2: Find a plugin for WordPress

Marketing purists will undoubtedly scoff at the previous suggestion to just use a spreadsheet, so here are a few other options. These are all free plugins for WordPress that offer some capabilities to manage newsletters. Some are more capable than others, but capability can also come with the price of added complexity:

- MeeNews Newsletter plugin: `http://wp-newsletter.com`
- MailPress: `http://www.mailpress.org`
- SendIt!: `http://www.giuseppesurace.com` (the site is in Italian, but the plugin is in English)

No, these are not the only newsletter plugin options, but they do work well and they host everything within WordPress. They are not simply extensions to a third-party service. All of these plugins could work well for sending a newsletter to any number of subscribers. Be warned though, depending on your web hosting setup, your host might think you are sending SPAM and temporarily disable your account.

Option 3: A third-party service

Finally, if you don't want the hassle of dealing with subscribers and worrying about getting your server flagged for supposedly sending SPAM, perhaps a third-party e-mail campaign monitor is for you.

If you choose to pay for one of these services, you can expect them to automatically manage all subscribes, unsubscribes, and e-mail bounces. You can also expect them to offer a variety of pre-formatted templates for your newsletters, plus provide detailed statistics about your campaign. All you need to do is sit back, type your letter, and let them handle the rest. Here are just a few of the available options:

- VerticalResponse: `http://www.verticalresponse.com`
- Benchmark Email: `http://www.benchmarkemail.com`
- Campaign Monitor: `http://www.campaignmonitor.com`

Prices may vary depending upon the services offered, but a standard base price is usually about a penny or two per subscriber per email sent. Naturally, this can get costly, but if you have enough subscribers to merit using a third-party service, chances are high that you will quickly make up for it with additional sales.

The creators of the WP e-Commerce plugin also have a WordPress plugin to tie into Campaign Monitor. Check it out at: http://www.instinct.co.nz/nextgen-wp-campaign-monitor.

Business blogging

Just a quick note here; there are entire books dedicated to business blogging. Don't forget that WordPress is designed first and foremost as a blogging tool. Sure, it's also powerful and flexible enough to become a great platform for e-commerce, but you already have a great tool at your disposal. Many other e-commerce sites have a blog as a "bolt-on" project, but WordPress offers seamless blog integration for you.

Depending upon the nature of your store, a business blog can be a powerful tool for attracting visitors and keeping them as repeat customers. Just as with a newsletter, you can publish announcements about upcoming products, sales, coupons, and anything else you think customers might care to see. Your blog could also contain funny anecdotes about products, detailed reviews, or other information related to your industry.

Establishing a business blog gives your store personality (a face behind the storefront). Use it to your advantage, and you can pick up more fans and followers.

Summary

Ultimately, the message here is that the more active you stay with the post-launch elements of your shop, the more likely you are to start accumulating visitors and customers. Just like how the human brain never wants to stop learning, a good store owner should never stop trying to improve the overall store, either by researching and creating new products, or by finding new ways to promote said products.

The difference between a successful person and an unsuccessful person is that the successful person does what the unsuccessful person was not willing to do: persevere and see a project through to the end. The marketing methods listed in this chapter are only a handful of the overall tactics that you can try. No single technique is "good enough," and a combination of many different techniques is what will eventually bring you success.

You make an investment when you build an e-commerce store, not just in money, but in time. The hours that you have put into building your shop are just planting the seed. That seed will need watering, fertilizer, and other care as it matures into a full grown plant. We manifest that ongoing care through our active participation in the health and growth of our stores. Especially in the early days, remember that every newsletter that you send, every blog post that you write, and every coupon that you spread to the world actively helps nurture and strengthen your seedling. With that continued care, your store will take root and pay rich dividends for the rest of your entrepreneurial life.

The topics that were covered in this chapter are:

- Coupons and discounts—details on setting both storewide discounts and per item coupons.
- Cross Sales—the art of suggesting other products that customers might like.
- Built-in 'Share This' plugin—if one social network is good, more is better. Allow your customers to advertise for you.
- Purchasing advertising—an overview of the Google AdWords and Microsoft adCenter networks.
- E-mail, newsletters, and blogging—several options for collecting newsletter subscriptions, setting up an email campaign, and venturing into business blogging.

Good luck, and heartfelt wishes for success for you and your e-commerce store!

Gold Cart Module Extendibility

The WP e-Commerce plugin comes in two different flavors: a free version and a "Gold" version. Whereas the vast majority of this book focuses on the free version, the Gold upgrade offers some additional features. One can easily run a successful shop without paying for the upgrade, but if you want to unlock certain features, such as product search, or want access to certain payment gateways, the Gold Cart Module is a worthy purchase.

We'll now take a look at the following details for the Gold Cart module:

- Purchasing and installing the Gold Cart module
- Grid View
- Multiple Image Upload
- Product Search Option
- Additional Payment Gateways
- DropShop and other modules

Purchasing and installing the Gold Cart module

At present, the Gold Cart upgrade has two pricing schemes: one for individual bloggers or hobbyists, and one for groups or businesses. What's the difference? The difference is only in the price, not in features or functionality. Individual store owners and non-profit organizations can purchase the **Single / Blogger** license. If your for-profit company has more than one staff member, you should opt for the **Business** license:

The current prices are $40 and $195 respectively.

Purchasing the Gold Cart upgrade gives you yet another chance to see the WP e-Commerce plugin in action, as Instinct Entertainment naturally uses it to power their own shopping cart. All transactions are handled through PayPal, so add your preferred package(s) to your cart and proceed to checkout:

Description	Unit Price	Quantity	Amount
Gold Cart & Grid Module (Single / Blogger - $40) Item # 1	$40.00	1	$40.00
		Item total:	$40.00
		Total:	**$40.00** USD

After you pay for your Gold Cart upgrade, PayPal will redirect you back to Instinct for your transaction results, which will provide you with your username, an API key, and a download link for the Gold Cart files:

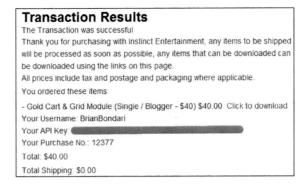

 If your files or purchase receipt do not arrive immediately, be sure to check your Spam folder in your e-mail.

Installing the Gold Cart files

Getting the Gold Cart up and running is a two-step process. First, we need to upload the Gold files to the appropriate place on our server. Next, we need to add our API Key information within the WordPress Dashboard.

Within the Gold Cart archive that you downloaded after your purchase, you will potentially find more than one version of upgrade files. As of this writing, the Gold Cart upgrade package contains files for both the latest version (3.7) and the previous version (3.6). Of course, you need concern yourself only with the files relevant to whichever version of the plugin you are currently running. For example, if you are using WP e-Commerce version 3.7, you can safely discard the 3.6 upgrade folder:

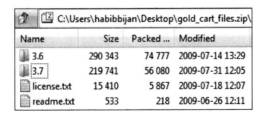

As we are running WP e-Commerce version 3.7, we can ignore any other folders inside the Gold Cart files archive. Within the 3.7 folder, we will find a readme file and another folder called `gold_cart_files`:

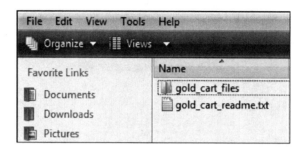

To install the Gold Cart, upload the entire `gold_cart_files` folder to your WordPress installation on your server using your favorite FTP program. The path is: `<your WordPress folder>/wp-content/uploads/wpsc/upgrades/`.

Here is a tree-layout of the directory structure with the Gold Cart files in their proper place:

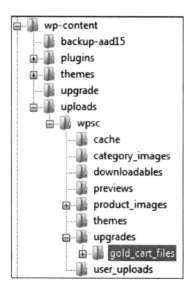

With the files uploaded correctly, we can now add our API Key information. Browse to your WordPress Dashboard and click on **Upgrades** under the **Products** menu:

The hard part is over. All we need to do now to complete the upgrade is add our username and API information that we received earlier. On the **Upgrades** page, you should now see a panel where you can add your unique username and API Key:

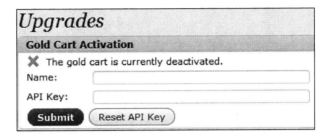

Click on the **Submit** button to validate your information. The additional Gold Cart features should now be unlocked and available to you:

Grid View

By upgrading to the Gold Cart, you have access to the Grid View layout, which provides you with another way to present your products to your customers. To enable Grid View, navigate to the **Presentation** tab for your WP e-Commerce settings. Part-way down the page you should see your **Product Page Settings**. With the Gold Cart unlocked, you can now select the **Grid View** option, plus configure additional layout tweaks for it:

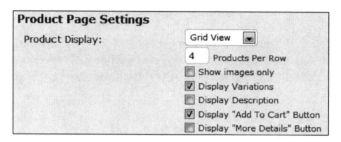

With Grid View active, your products will display in one or more rows, depending on how many products you have.

 If Grid View does not seem to work with some of your products, one suggestion is to ensure that you are not overriding your layout for a particular group with a differing pre-selected layout. You can look in Categories and edit your Group settings to make sure.

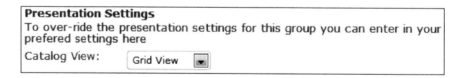

Multiple image upload

Another nice feature of the Gold Cart is that it unlocks access to a Flash-based upload tool for adding multiple images at once versus a single image at a time. This can save a lot of time if you have many images for each product that you sell. Once you have uploaded the images, you can also drag them to reorder the way in which they are displayed:

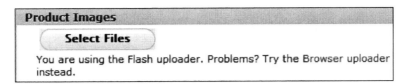

Product search option

At present, the free version of WP e-Commerce does not come with a product search feature. The ability to grant customers a way to search for specific products on your site is, unfortunately, one of the most-pressing reasons to upgrade to the Gold Cart. Every competing plugin to WP e-Commerce allows for product searching by default, even in their respective free versions, so it is unfortunate that the WP e-Commerce developers feel the need to relegate this necessary feature to the paid version (although they have every right to do so). Shop owners with large product catalogs will especially feel the need to upgrade to the Gold Cart as a result.

On the other hand, the Product Search feature that is unlocked when you buy the Gold Cart is very well done. It is more than a simple search box. It also offers some advanced searching capabilities as well as a slick *Live* search options, which automatically starts suggesting results as the customer types instead of waiting until the *Enter* key is pressed.

To enable Product Search, navigate to the **Presentation** tab under your WP e-Commerce settings. About halfway down the page, you will find a **Show Search** option:

When Search is enabled, you will now find an *Apple-esque* search box on all of your store pages:

Keep in mind that the WP e-Commerce Product Search feature only works for the products in your store. It does not also search your regular WordPress posts and pages. There is a third-party commercial plugin available to unify Product Search and WordPress search:
`http://embeddeddreams.com/users/njay/suniwpsc.php`

Additional payment gateways

Looking for more payment processors than those bundled with the standard version of the shopping cart? Another boon to having the Gold Cart unlocked is that you now have access to a plethora of additional payment gateways. The most notable addition is Authorize.net. Some of the other gateways include: eWay, DPS, iDeal, Sagepay, Linkpoint, and Bluepay:

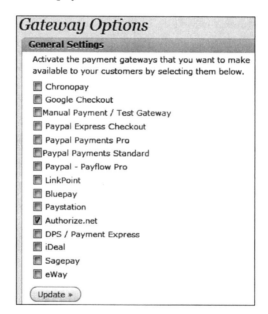

DropShop and other modules

The Gold Cart comes with some impressive, and in some cases, necessary features. However, there are additional modules available that unlock features above and beyond those of the Gold Cart. If you want access to them, you must buy them individually.

Of the additional modules, the most notable (and expensive) is undoubtedly DropShop. When enabled, DropShop adds an elegant AJAX shopping cart to the footer of your WordPress shop. Customers can add items to the cart simply by dragging and dropping them there:

DropShop is certainly impressive, but so is the price, which is currently $100. You must already own the Gold Cart in order for DropShop to work.

Most of the other available modules serve a much more specific purpose, and all of them are comparatively less expensive. These additional modules include:

- **MP3 Audio Player** — useful for a music store owner who wants to provide previews of audio files before purchase. The current price is $10.
- **Product Slider** — adds a scrollable display unit for quickly browsing through a number of products. The current price is $25.
- **Members Only** — useful if you want to charge for private access to posts, pages, galleries, podcasts, or forums. The current price is $25.
- **NextGEN Gallery 'Buy Now' Buttons** — for use in conjunction with the NextGEN Gallery plugin (adds a 'Buy Now' button to each image in the gallery). The current price is $10.

Summary

Once again, it is entirely possible to run a successful web shop with only the free version of the WP e-Commerce plugin. However, the Gold Upgrade is a reasonably priced upgrade that offers a lot of useful amenities. For an active shop, especially one with a growing product catalog, the Gold Cart is a useful upgrade, granting access to Product Search, Grid View, multiple image upload, and a slew of new payment gateways.

For store owners who want even more features, specific modules are available to address those needs.

B
Setting Up a WAMP Testing Platform

One strong recommendation is to create a testing ground in which to install WordPress and the WP e-Commerce plugin that is independent from your production server. That way you can test, and re-test, any changes without fear of breaking your live site.

Turning your personal computer into a testing platform is simple. We only need a few different tools in order to create a development environment, including:

- A web server, such as Apache
- A database server, such as MySQL
- PHP
- Supporting libraries

Fortunately, a few free software packages exist that bundle all of these tools together into one centralized program. For the Microsoft Windows operating system, these packages include:

- WampServer (http://www.wampserver.com/en)
- XAMPP (http://www.apachefriends.org/en/xampp.html)
- Microsoft Web Platform (http://www.microsoft.com/Web/)

In this section, we will discuss the installation, setup, and basic usage of WampServer.

Download and install WampServer

First things first, let's download the WampServer package. Visit the URL mentioned on the previous page and click on the **Downloads** link. This will yield a page displaying a link to the latest available package:

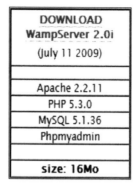

Once the file finishes downloading, it's time to install it. Launch the executable, and just like installing any other software program on Windows, follow the prompts to complete the installation.

You must have administrative privileges to install WampServer.

The installation prompts are straightforward, and the only issue you need to consider is the installation directory. By default, the installation path is c:\wamp, and this is the recommended location:

At the end of the installation, you will be prompted to choose the browser that you would like to have WampServer automatically launch whenever you access your test site. By default, Internet Explorer is already chosen for you, but you can pick any other installed browser.

When the program launches for the first time, any software firewall that you are running will likely prompt you for a security alert. This is expected behavior as the Apache web server requires access to Port 80 on your computer. Therefore, you can safely unblock it. You will also be prompted for **PHP mail parameters**. Our testing ground has no real need for this, so we can safely click on **Next**:

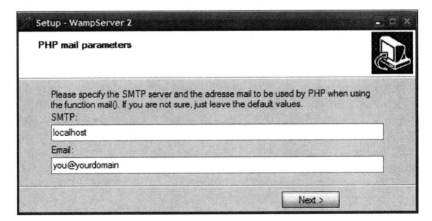

At this point, WampServer should be successfully installed and running.

Overview and configuration

When WampServer is running, you will see its icon in your system tray. To access its services at any time, just click on the icon to display the full menu:

Notice that the menu expands for **Apache**, **PHP**, and **MySQL**. If you ever need to add or edit components, or gain quick access to the main configuration files for each service, you can do so there.

 The **Put Online** option is *not* necessary for our development work. In fact, it is dangerous to enable this option without tightening the security of the various services. Putting WampServer online will make your computer accessible on your local network and possibly over the Internet, creating a potentially serious security risk.

Enable the rewrite module

Though not necessarily required, it's a good idea to enable the `rewrite_module` within the Apache web server. This module allows Apache to rewrite URLs so they look more practical and SEO-friendly. WordPress relies on the `rewrite_module` to alter the structure of permalinks.

To enable this module, open the WampServer menu and browse to **Apache**, then **Apache modules**. Select the **rewrite_module**:

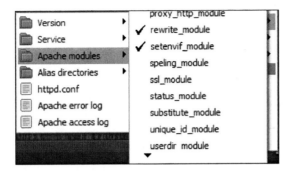

We're now ready to install WordPress on our test server.

Running a test server

Our testing platform is now fully operational as a development server. The only thing missing is WordPress itself, so let's add it now.

First, let's create a new empty database. From the WampServer menu, launch **phpMyAdmin**. Under the **MySQL localhost** section, type a name for your new database and click on the **Create** button:

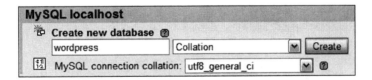

Install WordPress

To install WordPress, download the software package from `www.wordpress.org`. The archive that you download contains a folder called `wordpress`. Extract that folder and its contents to the `www` folder inside the location where you decided to install WampServer. If you chose the default location, the full path will be `C:\wamp\www`:

Next, navigate into your `wordpress` folder. Find the file called `wp-config-sample.php` and rename it to `wp-config.php`. Naturally, this file contains the configuration details for properly installing WordPress.

You now need to open the `wp-config.php` file with a text editor (such as Notepad) and change a few details:

- Database name—`wordpress` (or whatever name you entered in the previous step)
- Database username—`root`
- Database password—leave it blank
- Hostname—`localhost`

That's all! Remember that these settings are for development and testing purposes only. You definitely should not open WampServer to your network, or to the Internet, without securing it further.

You are now ready to complete the install of WordPress. In your browser, navigate to `http://localhost/wordpress/wp-admin/install.php` and follow the short prompts, just as in any other typical WordPress installation.

You're finished!

Summary

WampServer is a fantastic and simple way to test your WordPress shop before changes are rolled to your production server. It's free, open source, flexible, and easy to use. By using a testing platform, we can experiment to our heart's content with both WordPress and the WP e-Commerce plugin without fear of breaking anything on the live site.

Index

Packt Open Source Project Royalties

When we sell a book written on an Open Source project, we pay a royalty directly to that project. Therefore by purchasing WordPress 2.9 e-Commerce, Packt will have given some of the money received to the WordPress project.

In the long term, we see ourselves and you—customers and readers of our books—as part of the Open Source ecosystem, providing sustainable revenue for the projects we publish on. Our aim at Packt is to establish publishing royalties as an essential part of the service and support a business model that sustains Open Source.

If you're working with an Open Source project that you would like us to publish on, and subsequently pay royalties to, please get in touch with us.

Writing for Packt

We welcome all inquiries from people who are interested in authoring. Book proposals should be sent to author@packtpub.com. If your book idea is still at an early stage and you would like to discuss it first before writing a formal book proposal, contact us; one of our commissioning editors will get in touch with you.

We're not just looking for published authors; if you have strong technical skills but no writing experience, our experienced editors can help you develop a writing career, or simply get some additional reward for your expertise.

About Packt Publishing

Packt, pronounced 'packed', published its first book "Mastering phpMyAdmin for Effective MySQL Management" in April 2004 and subsequently continued to specialize in publishing highly focused books on specific technologies and solutions.

Our books and publications share the experiences of your fellow IT professionals in adapting and customizing today's systems, applications, and frameworks. Our solution-based books give you the knowledge and power to customize the software and technologies you're using to get the job done. Packt books are more specific and less general than the IT books you have seen in the past. Our unique business model allows us to bring you more focused information, giving you more of what you need to know, and less of what you don't.

Packt is a modern, yet unique publishing company, which focuses on producing quality, cutting-edge books for communities of developers, administrators, and newbies alike. For more information, please visit our website: www.PacktPub.com.

WordPress 2.7 Cookbook

ISBN: 978-1-847197-38-2   Paperback: 316 pages

100 simple but incredibly useful recipes to take control of your WordPress blog layout, themes, widgets, plug-ins, security, and SEO

1. Take your WordPress blog to the next level with solutions to common WordPress problems that make your blog better, smarter, faster, and more secure

2. Enhance your SEO and make more money online by applying simple hacks

3. Fully tested and compatible with WordPress 2.7

WordPress Plugin Development: Beginner's Guide

ISBN: 978-1-847193-59-9   Paperback: 296 pages

Build powerful, interactive plug-ins for your blog and to share online

1. Everything you need to create and distribute your own plug-ins following WordPress coding standards

2. Walk through the development of six complete, feature-rich, real-world plug-ins that are being used by thousands of WP users

3. Written by Vladimir Prelovac, WordPress expert and developer of WordPress plug-ins such as Smart YouTube and Plugin Central

Please check **www.PacktPub.com** for information on our titles

WordPress 2.7 Complete

ISBN: 978-1-847196-56-9   Paperback: 296 pages

Create your own complete blog or web site from
scratch with WordPress

1. Everything you need to set up your own
   feature-rich WordPress blog or web site

2. Clear and practical explanations of all aspects
   of WordPress

3. In-depth coverage of installation, themes,
   syndication, and podcasting

4. Explore WordPress as a fully functioning
   content management system

WordPress Theme Design

ISBN: 978-1-847193-09-4   Paperback: 224 pages

A complete guide to creating professional
WordPress themes

1. Take control of the look and feel of your
   WordPress site

2. Simple, clear tutorial to creating Unique and
   Beautiful themes

3. Expert guidance with practical step-by-step
   instructions for theme design

4. Design tips, tricks, and troubleshooting ideas

Please check **www.PacktPub.com** for information on our titles

LaVergne, TN USA
01 March 2011
218281LV00003B/41/P